DOR
& CA

writing
PARAGRAPHS
FROM SENTENCE TO PARAGRAPH

MACMILLAN

Contents

To the Teacher

Writing is an important form of communication in day-to-day life, but it is especially important in high school and university. Writing is also one of the most difficult skills to master in both a first language and a second language. Students can find it challenging to find ideas to include in their writing, and each culture has its own style for organizing academic writing. However, with the help of this book and your guidance, your students will learn to recognize good academic paragraphs and develop their own paragraph writing skills.

This new edition of *Writing Paragraphs* is designed to help low-intermediate students analyze model paragraphs, find ideas for their writing, put their ideas into sentences, organize their sentences into paragraphs, review their paragraphs, and revise their paragraphs so that they become even stronger. This process approach to writing will not only develop your students' paragraph writing skills, but will also encourage them to become independent and creative writers.

Each main unit provides an interesting theme to engage your students and motivate them to read and analyze the model paragraphs. The unit themes also inspire your students to create their own writing. An introductory unit shows students how to format their writing and introduces the idea of process writing.

The activities in each unit help students with a particular aspect of paragraph writing, such as brainstorming, writing topic sentences, and developing paragraphs with supporting sentences. A unit's activities might also teach correct punctuation for academic writing and useful grammatical functions for writing, such as conjunctions and connecting words and expressions. The units also show students how to review their own and their classmates' writing in order to make revisions.

Each unit ends with a structured writing assignment that provides an opportunity for students to use everything presented in the unit. Included in the Student Book are samples of a paragraph from brainstorming to final draft, with a completed Peer Review Form. There is also a guide to common grammatical terms and concepts useful for writers, and a guide to punctuation for easy reference.

The Teacher's Guide supports the instructor by offering teaching suggestions, a discussion of marking and grading writing, ideas for supplemental activities for each unit, and answers to exercises in the Student Book.

Learning to write well takes a lot of practice and patience. Students need clear guidance, positive feedback, and interesting ideas to write about. We hope this book provides this for you and you enjoy using it.

To the Student

Writing is a very important part of your school and university study. You will write assignments that may be one paragraph or several paragraphs, and you will write answers for tests and exams that may be a few sentences, a paragraph or two, or a complete essay.

Academic writing in English may be different not only from academic writing in your own language, but even from other writing in English. The purpose of this new edition of *Writing Paragraphs* is to help you recognize and produce the sort of paragraph writing that will be expected of you in academic situations.

During this course, you will have many opportunities to study and discuss examples of English academic paragraph writing. You will also have many opportunities to discuss your own paragraphs and the paragraphs of your classmates. You will learn how important the reader is to the writer, and how to express clearly and directly what you mean to communicate. We hope that what you learn in this course will help you throughout your academic studies and beyond.

You should come to your writing class every day with energy and a willingness to work and learn. Your instructor and your classmates have much to share with you, and you have much to share with them. By coming to class with your questions, taking chances and trying new ways, and expressing your ideas in another language, you will add not only to your own world, but to the world of those around you.

Good luck!

Dorothy E Zemach
Carlos Islam

Introduction

In this unit, you will learn ...
- formatting for handwritten and word-processed assignments.
- how to write headings.
- about process writing.

Formatting

I Look at these student papers. Check (✓) the ones that have the correct form for an academic assignment.

⊃ Handwritten

a. ☐

I think students should wear uniforms to school. They cost less money than regular clothes. Everybody looks the same, so students can think about schoolwork instead of their looks. In addition,

b. ☐

I think students should wear uniforms to school. They cost less money than regular clothes. Everybody looks the same, so students can think about schoolwork instead of their looks.

In addition,

c. ☐

I think students should wear uniforms to school. They cost less money than regular clothes. Everybody looks the same, so students can think about schoolwork instead of their looks. In addition,

⊃ Word-processed

a. ☐

School uniforms are not good for students. They are not attractive, so students feel bad when they are wearing them. Students like to express their personalities by choosing their own clothes.

b. ☐

School uniforms are not good for students. They are not attractive, so students feel bad when they are wearing them. Students like to express their personalities by choosing their own clothes.

c. ☐

School uniforms are not good for students. They are not attractive, so students feel bad when they are wearing them. Students like to express their personalities by choosing their own clothes.

d. ☐

School uniforms are not good for students. They are not attractive, so students feel bad when they are wearing them. Students like to express their personalities by choosing their own clothes.

2 **Look at these different ways of writing headings for student papers. Answer the questions below.**

a.

> Karen Chou
> Professor Miller
> English Writing 1
> April 12, 2011
>
>   School Uniforms Are Good

1. What is the writer's name?

2. What is the name of the class?

3. Who is teaching the class?

4. What is the title of the assignment?

b.

>   Sebastian Mitchell
>   School uniforms
>   2nd draft
>   September 5, 2011
>
>   Students Should Choose Their Own Clothes

1. What is the writer's name?

2. What is the title of the assignment?

3. What is the assignment about?

4. What does "2nd draft" mean?

5. When did the writer write the assignment?

How does your teacher want you to write headings in this class?

Write an example here:

Process writing

3   Take a quiz! First guess the correct answers. Then read the paragraphs below to check your guesses.

a. "Process writing" means

☐ writing in English.
☐ writing with a word processor.
☐ writing in several stages (steps).

b. Before you begin to write, you should

☐ finish the homework for your other classes.
☐ get some ideas.
☐ ask your friends for help.

c. Your teacher may ask you to read a classmate's paper and answer some questions about it. This is because

☐ you can learn a lot by reading your classmate's assignment.
☐ your teacher is too busy to read all the students' papers.
☐ you are a better writer than your classmate.

d. Your teacher may ask you to write another draft. This is because

☐ your teacher can't think of any new assignments.
☐ the first time, your paper was bad.
☐ you can make your paper better by making some changes.

e. Before you hand in your paper for a grade, you should

☐ ask your teacher to give you a good grade.
☐ check it carefully.
☐ put some pretty stickers on it.

a. Musicians practice their pieces many times before a concert. Athletes work out before a competition. In the same way, good writers go through several stages when they write. "Process writing" will guide you through these stages so your final paper is really your effort.

b. The first stage of process writing is getting ideas. In this course, you will learn and practice several different ways to get ideas. Try them all and see which way works best for you.

c. An important stage in process writing is sharing your writing. You can see how other writers like you handled the same assignment, and you can get some good ideas from them. You can also see how well someone else understands your ideas.

d. After you finish your assignment, put it away for some time. When you look at it again, you may have new ideas. Your classmates may help you find new ideas, too. Writing your paper again (called "revising") gives you the chance to improve your paper.

e. Before you give your teacher your paper, check it carefully. Read it out loud. Does it sound natural? Did you forget any words? Did you remember to write the heading correctly? Does your paper look neat? Remember to give your teacher your best effort!

Beginning to Work

In this unit, you will ...

■ recognize and write complete sentences.

■ learn how to begin and end a sentence.

■ learn the common features of a paragraph.

■ identify the topic of a paragraph.

■ identify strong and weak paragraphs.

1 Look at this chart. Check (✓) the answers for your country.

	It's common.	It's not common.	I'm not sure. / It depends.
a. High school students have part-time jobs.	☐	☐	☐
b. University students have part-time jobs.	☐	☐	☐
c. University students have volunteer jobs (jobs that don't pay a salary).	☐	☐	☐
d. Part-time jobs pay a good salary.	☐	☐	☐
e. After graduation, both men and women want to find a full-time job.	☐	☐	☐

2 Share your information with a group of your classmates. Ask and answer these questions about part-time jobs.

- What are common part-time jobs?
- Have you ever had a job? What was your first job?
- What kind of job do you think is best for a high school / university student?
- (your idea)

3 You are going to read a paragraph called *Part-time Jobs and High School*. What do you think the paragraph is about? Circle the answer.

   a. Useful high school subjects

   b. Working and studying at the same time

   c. How much money a part-time job pays

4 Read the paragraph. Did you choose the right answer in exercise 3 above?

Part-time Jobs and High School

[1] High school students should not have part-time jobs. [2] High school is a very important time for a student, and students are very busy. [3] Students have to study hard to enter a good university. [4] Many high school students also play sports, and they practice before and after school. [5] High school students also spend time with friends of the same age. [6] Those friendships can be important for the rest of their lives. [7] A part-time job takes time away from studying, playing sports, and making friends. [8] People work for most of their adult lives. [9] When they are in high school, it's important for them to just be high school students.

5 Which sentence tells the writer's most important idea?

   1 ☐   2 ☐   3 ☐   8 ☐

6 What do sentences 3, 4, and 5 do?

   a. They show new ideas.

   b. They give examples.

   c. They show different opinions.

7 Do you agree with the writer? Why / Why not?

Writing focus: What is a sentence?

How many words are in the shortest English sentence? Except for one-word commands (*Sit!*), a complete sentence in English needs two words: a subject (a noun or pronoun) and a predicate (a verb) (*She sits*).

Of course, most English sentences are longer than just two words, but every sentence tells a complete thought. Groups of words that do not make complete sentences are called *phrases*.

If you need more information on complete sentences and phrases, see pages 85–87.

8 **Work with a partner. Look at the following. Some of them could be sentences with the correct punctuation. Check (✓) the ones that could be sentences.**

   a. ☐ housewives and young parents

   b. ☐ some retired people want to work

   c. ☐ earn some extra money

   d. ☐ meet new people

   e. ☐ volunteer jobs don't pay a salary

   f. ☐ an opportunity to learn new skills

   g. ☐ several part-time jobs

Language focus: Capital letters and final punctuation

Sentences in a paragraph ...

- start with a capital letter
  Part-time jobs can be stressful.

- end with a period (.) question mark (?) or exclamation point (!)
  Many students work as tutors.
  How old were you when you got your first job?
  I will never work in a restaurant again!

Note: Exclamation points are not as common in academic writing as they are in casual writing. Don't use them too often. Never use more than one exclamation point at the end of a sentence in academic writing.

The company offered me a part-time job!! = when writing to friends

The company offered me a part-time job. = when writing in school

9 Unscramble the sentences and write them on the lines below. Begin and end each sentence correctly.

a. in a shop / my sister / works

    My sister works in a shop...

b. is / a useful subject / computer science

    ....

c. don't / I / like / working with people

    ....

d. can't find / many students / a job / easily

    ....

e. more women / are / after college / working ?

    ....

f. first job / was / my / wonderful / a / experience

    ....

10 Look again at exercise 8 on page 7. Write the complete sentences with correct punctuation. Add to the phrases to make complete sentences. Then share your sentences with a partner. How are they different?

a. ....

b. ....

c. ....

d. ....

e. ....

f. ....

g. ....

Writing focus: What is a paragraph?

A paragraph is a group of about 6–12 sentences about one *topic*. Every sentence in a strong paragraph is about the same topic. All of the sentences explain the writer's *main idea* (most important idea) about that topic. When the writer wants to write about a new main idea, he / she begins a new paragraph.

A paragraph can give information, tell an opinion, explain something, or even tell a short story. The sentences are arranged logically, so the reader can easily understand what the writer wants to say.

In academic writing, a paragraph has a *topic sentence* that directly tells the reader the main idea. The other sentences in the paragraph, called *supporting sentences*, give more information about the topic. They add specific details and explanations. In academic English, the topic sentence is usually (but not always!) first or last.

1 Work with a partner. Read the groups of sentences below and on page 10. Circle the letters of the strong paragraphs. If you think the sentences make a weak paragraph, say why. Choose one or more of these reasons:

- The sentences are not all about the same topic.

- There are not enough sentences.

- There is no topic sentence.

- Some sentences say the same thing.

When I need a good place to study, I go to the library. It's always quiet there, so I can concentrate. It's easy to find the books I need, and I can search for information on the Internet because there are several computers. The other people in the library are also reading or working, so the mood is good for studying. I study better and faster in the library than in any other place.

a. ....
....

I need to buy a motorcycle. With a motorcycle, I could get to my job more quickly. It takes two hours to get to work by train. That's very slow. A motorcycle is much faster. If I had a motorcycle, I could save a lot of time. Taking the train is not fast enough for me.

b. ....
....

> First, insert a blank CD into the computer. Then, select the song list that you want to copy. You will see a button that says, "Click here to burn." Click on that button. Then just wait a few minutes. That's all!

c. ....

....

> *I will never forget my first day of high school. I was very nervous because I didn't know any of the other students. In my first class, I looked around for someone friendly. I saw a girl at the front of the room who also looked nervous, so I decided to make friends with her. Even though I was shy about talking to her, I went up to her and said, "Don't be nervous. I will help you. Do you want to sit with me?" She looked a little surprised and said, "Actually, I am the new teacher."*

d. ....

....

> Smart phones are very popular. They're convenient. They have a lot of applications.

e. ....

....

> Sports instructor is a good part-time job. You can enjoy your favorite activity and earn money at the same time. Some other jobs pay better. You can also volunteer as an instructor. I had a difficult time learning to swim, because my instructor wasn't very good. My tennis instructor was much better. If you get a lot of experience as a sports instructor, you can get a job at a gym or as a coach in the future.

f. ....

....

12 Read this paragraph about a student's first job. What is the topic?

   a. Working in a laboratory

   b. Getting my first job

   c. What my first job taught me

Learning Responsibility

[1] My first job was as a sales clerk in a small clothing store. [2] It wasn't a difficult job, and it wasn't really a very interesting job. [3] My best friend had a more exciting job. [4] Every weekend I had to open the store at 10:00 a.m. [5] I couldn't be late. [6] Now on weekends I like to sleep late. [7] I helped customers find clothes, and I kept the store neat and clean. [8] My parents' house was very clean, too. [9] I used the cash register and handled credit cards, so I had to be very careful. [10] These things all taught me responsibility. [11] Now I work in a research laboratory. [12] I don't work with clothing anymore, but I still use that important skill I learned in my first job.

---

13 Cross out the sentences that are not connected to the topic.

14 Which additional sentences could be connected to the paragraph? Write C (connected) or U (unconnected).

   a. .... I answered the phone and opened the mail.

   b. .... On weekdays I did my homework for school.

   c. .... I once worked delivering pizza, too.

   d. .... I learned how to choose and order new clothing.

   e. .... Dressing neatly and professionally was an important part of the job.

   f. .... A lab assistant is a good job for me.

   g. .... In the future, I would like to take some business trips.

1

Put it together

a Look at these sentences for a paragraph about having a part-time job in high school. Cross out the ones that are not connected. On a separate sheet of paper, write a paragraph using the connected sentences. They are already in the right order but are not yet correctly punctuated.

having a part-time job is a valuable experience for American high school students

they can learn many things that are not usually taught in a classroom

for example, they can learn how to work with older people

I was the youngest person in my high school class

they also get experience with the business world

I took a business class in college that was very good

having a part-time job gives students a sense of independence

they can also earn money to use for college

college tuition in the U.S. is more expensive than in many other countries

education is more than just school subjects

learning about the real world is also important

some colleges help their graduates find jobs after graduation

b Check your writing.
Did you ...
- [ ] include a heading on your paper?
- [ ] format the paragraph properly (see page 2)?
- [ ] start and end each sentence correctly?
- [ ] give the paragraph a title?

c Hand in your paragraph to your teacher.

2 Giving and Receiving Gifts

In this unit, you will ...
- identify topics and main ideas.
- identify strong and weak topic sentences.
- practice writing topic sentences.
- combine sentences using *and* and *but*.
- learn how to use commas in sentences with *and* and *but*.

I Tell a partner about the last gift you received.
- Who gave you the gift?
- When did they give you the gift?
- What was the gift? Did you like it?

2 Read the paragraph and answer the questions.

a. What is the topic of the paragraph?
  1. celebrating birthdays
  2. the writer's family
  3. choosing gifts

b. What is the writer's most important opinion about the topic?
  1. Gifts should be old.
  2. Gifts should be chosen carefully.
  3. A photograph is a good birthday gift.

c. Why does the writer like the photograph?
  1. It helps him think about his father.
  2. It wasn't expensive.
  3. It was a birthday gift.

A Birthday Gift

[1] Choosing a birthday gift for a friend or family member is fun, but it can be difficult. [2] The gift should be personal and has to be thoughtful. [3] For example, the best birthday gift I ever got wasn't fancy or expensive. [4] Last year my mother gave me a photograph of my father when he was my age. [5] He is standing with his mother and father (my grandparents) in front of their house, and he looks happy. [6] I think of my father every time I see that photo. [7] It was a perfect birthday gift.

Writing focus: Topic sentences

A good topic sentence should include either of the following:

- one clear topic
  weak: *It's important to have friends, and also to do well in school.*
  strong: *I don't think I will ever have a better friend than Heather.*

- an opinion or idea about the topic
  weak: *I have been studying karate.*
  strong: *Studying karate has given me strength and self-confidence.*

A good topic sentence should **not** be:

- too *broad* (too much to write about)
  weak: *Australia is an interesting country.*
  strong: *On my visit to Australia, I saw many unusual animals.*

- too *narrow* (not enough to write about / is just a fact)
  weak: *School starts at 8:30 a.m.*
  strong: *Getting ready for school in the morning is more difficult than any of my classes.*

Remember: The topic sentence is *usually* the first or last sentence, but it can be any sentence in the paragraph.

3   **Look at these topic sentences. Circle the topic of the sentence. Underline the main idea.**

   a. This (soccer ball) was <u>the gift I liked best.</u>

   b. Shopping for gifts online takes a lot of time.

   c. The last CD I received changed my life.

   d. There are three reasons why I want a new laptop.

   e. Reading novels, such as the *Twilight* series, can help students improve their English.

   f. A present tells you a lot about the person who bought it.

   g. An amusement park was the perfect place to hold our graduation party.

4   **Look again at the paragraph on page 13, *A Birthday Gift*. Which sentence is the topic sentence? Circle the topic and underline the main idea.**

5   In the following pairs, circle the number of the best topic sentence. Then explain your choice to a partner. Say why the sentence you didn't choose is weak. Use one or more of these reasons:

- It's too broad.

- It's too narrow.

- There is no main idea or opinion.

- There is more than one main idea.

a. **1.** Gifts can cost a lot of money, and then you also have to wrap them.

(**2.**) Wrapping a gift in a special way can make your gift seem even more special.

There are two main ideas.

b. **1.** Receiving gifts can make some people feel uncomfortable.

2. I really like gifts.

....

c. **1.** Parents spend too much money on birthday gifts for babies.

2. For my last birthday, I got a gold watch with a leather band from my father.

....

d. **1.** Different countries all over the world have interesting gift-giving customs.

2. Several gift-giving customs in China surprised me when I lived there.

....

e. **1.** The best gift I ever gave didn't cost me anything.

2. I spent €130 on a gift for my parents.

....

f. **1.** Shopping online makes it easier to find an appropriate gift.

2. Buying gifts online can be a good way to save money, but then sometimes you spend more money that way.

....

g. **1.** There are many proverbs in English.

2. There are several proverbs in English about gift-giving.

....

6 Improve these topic sentences. Circle the topic. Choose a main idea for each topic and write a topic sentence. Then share your new sentences with a partner or small group.

a. I have a (photo of my girlfriend.)

idea: *The photo reminds me of her.*

topic sentence: *I carry a photo of my girlfriend to remind me of her.*

b. I have a new jacket.

idea: ....

topic sentence: ....

c. The Internet is good.

idea: ....

topic sentence: ....

d. My friend is nice.

idea: ....

topic sentence: ....

e. I learn English at school.

idea: ....

topic sentence: ....

Language focus: Using and and but to join sentences

7 Work with a partner. Look at these pairs of sentences. How are they similar? How are they different? Which do you like better, and why?

a. 1. I sent my mother a birthday card. I called her.

   2. I sent my mother a birthday card and called her.

b. 1. I like getting flowers. I don't like getting candy.

   2. I like getting flowers, but I don't like getting candy.

c. 1. I didn't send my brother a birthday gift. He didn't send me one.

   2. I didn't send my brother a birthday gift, and he didn't send me one.

- In each case, the sentences in 2 *flow* better—that is, they sound more fluent and natural.

- Sentences about the same topic can often be combined with words like *and* and *but*.

- Use *and* to join *similar* ideas. In 7a, the writer did two things for her mother's birthday (sent a card; called her). How are the actions in 7c similar?

- Use *but* to show *contrasting* ideas: good / bad, easy / difficult, positive / negative. What is the contrast in 7b?

8 Look again at the paragraph on page 13, *A Birthday Gift*. Underline the sentences joined by *and* and *but*.

9 Complete this paragraph with *and* or *but*.

Same Holiday, Different Customs

People in the United States and Japan celebrate Valentine's Day on February 14. However, the holiday is celebrated in different ways in each country. In the U.S., Valentine's Day is enjoyed by friends and romantic partners, ª· .... in Japan usually only romantic partners celebrate this day. Chocolate is the most popular gift in Japan, ᵇ· .... it is common in the U.S. too. However, in the U.S., other kinds of gifts are also given, ᶜ· .... many people exchange cards. The biggest difference is that in Japan, girls and women give chocolate to boys and men, ᵈ· .... in the U.S., boys and girls give cards or small gifts to all of their friends. American men and women give gifts and cards to each other. In fact, women usually get more expensive gifts than men. I would like to be a man in Japan, ᵉ· .... a woman in the U.S.!

Note: Don't begin sentences with *And* or *But* in academic writing. Use *In addition* or *However* instead.

Language focus: Punctuation

When you join two complete sentences with *but*, you must always use a comma before *but*:

I didn't want to send her a gift. I sent her one anyway.

I didn't want to send her a gift, but I sent her one anyway.

When you join two complete sentences with *and* and the subjects of the sentences are both written, use a comma before *and*:

Shopping at the mall is expensive. Parking is hard to find.

Shopping at the mall is expensive, and parking is hard to find.

(*Shopping* and *parking* are both written.)

When you join two complete sentences and remove the subject of the second sentence, don't use a comma before *and*:

These days people mail paper cards. People e-mail electronic cards.

These days people mail paper cards and e-mail electronic cards.

These days people send paper and electronic cards.

(The subject *people* is not written a second time.)

10 Join these sentences with *and* or *but*. Use a comma if you need one. Then share your sentences with a partner. Did you make the same choices? Talk about any differences.

a. I got a camera for my birthday. I got clothes for Christmas.

I got a camera for my birthday, and I got clothes for Christmas.

I got a camera for my birthday and clothes for Christmas.

b. Ahmed speaks English very well. He enjoys his classes.

....

c. Yoshi studies hard. He doesn't get good grades.

....

d. In Asia, most people eat rice for breakfast. In Canada, most people have cereal.

....

e. Morocco has lovely mountains. Morocco has beautiful beaches.

....

f. Spanish is spoken in most of South America. Portuguese is spoken in Brazil.

....

g. Gifts are difficult to choose. Gifts are fun to give.

....

h. Noodles are easy to cook. Noodles are popular in many countries.

....

Put it together

a   Make a quick list of gifts you have given and received.

Gifts given   Gifts received

....

....

....

....

b   Choose one gift. Tell your partner about it. Ask and answer questions like these.

Gifts given

- Who gave it to you?
- When did you receive it?
- Why did someone choose that gift for you?
- What did you think of the gift?
- (your ideas)

Gifts received

- Who did you give it to?
- When did you give it?
- Why did you choose this gift?
- What did your friend or family member think of the gift you gave?
- (your ideas)

c   On a separate sheet of paper, write a topic sentence about your gift, and then write sentences with *and* and *but*.

d   Exchange papers with a partner.

- Circle your partner's topic and underline the main idea.
- Circle the commas your partner used.
- Talk with your partner and decide if your commas are in the right places.

e   Hand in your sentences to your teacher.

3 A Favorite Place

In this unit, you will ...
- develop paragraphs with descriptive details.
- use lists to brainstorm.
- learn to edit lists.
- combine sentences containing adjectives.
- write about places.

I Describe this picture to a partner. Have you been to the beach before? Tell your partner what it was like.

2 Read the paragraph and answer the questions on page 21 with a partner.

Relaxing at the Beach

[1] Where is your favorite summer vacation place? [2] The beach is the perfect place for me. [3] The air is hot, but the water is cool, wet, and fresh. [4] First, I enjoy swimming and surfing in the ocean. [5] When I am tired, I come out and lie on the beach. [6] The sand is soft and white. [7] The beach is noisy with seagulls and children laughing, but it's a pleasant noise. [8] I even like the beach smells. [9] The air smells salty from the sea and sweet from everybody's suntan lotion. [10] I feel peaceful and relaxed. [11] When I want to relax in summer, I go to the beach!

---

a. Which sentence is the topic sentence?

1 ☐   2 ☐   10 ☐

b. What do sentences 3, 4, 6, 7, and 9 do?

  1. Say the same information in a different way.

  2. Tell a story about the topic.

  3. Explain the topic sentence by giving more information.

Language focus: Descriptive vocabulary

You know that a topic sentence tells the main idea of a paragraph. *Supporting sentences* develop the paragraph by adding more information. When you describe a place, you can develop your paragraph by adding descriptive details—information that tells how a place looks, sounds, or smells, or feels.

3 With a partner, put these adjectives that can describe places into the chart below. Some words can be used in more than one place. Check a dictionary or ask your teacher to explain any new words.

dark	friendly	musical	soft
dry	green	quiet	spicy
exciting	humid	relaxed	sweet
fragrant	loud	sharp	warm

look	sound	smell	feel
....	....	....	....
....	....	....	....
....	....	....	....
....	....	....	....
....	....	....	....
....	....	....	....
....	....	....	....
....	....	....	....

4 Look again at the paragraph on page 20, *Relaxing at the Beach*. Circle the descriptive adjectives, and then put them into the chart in exercise 3 above.

Brainstorming: Lists

You cannot write if you don't have something to write about. So, before they start to write, good writers *brainstorm* ideas (they think of and write down ideas that they can use).

In this book, you will practice several different ways of brainstorming. Try them all, and then choose the way that works best for you.

↻ How to make a list

- Use a separate, whole sheet of paper.
- Write your topic at the top.
- Write down as many ideas as you can about your topic.
- Write single words or short phrases, but don't write long sentences.
- Write down every idea that comes to you, and don't worry about whether the ideas are "good" or "bad."

↻ Editing your list

After you brainstorm, you need to go back and see which ideas you can use. This is called *editing*.

- Underline or highlight the good ideas.
- Cross out ideas that are not related to your topic or that you don't want to use.

5 This example shows a list for the paragraph on page 20, *Relaxing at the Beach*. Cross out the ideas that the writer didn't use. Compare your list with a partner, and say why you think the writer didn't use the crossed out ideas.

6 Choose one of the topics below. In five minutes, make a list of ideas. Share your list with a partner. How many descriptive adjectives did your partner use?

   a. My favorite place to relax

   b. An interesting city

7 Edit your list by crossing out unrelated ideas or ones you don't like. Show your partner what you crossed out, and explain your decisions.

Beach

vacation

relax

air—hot, dry, windy?

water—cold, cool, fresh, wet

swim, surf

can't windsurf

seagulls

good snack food

beach umbrellas / expensive to rent

too far away

smell—salt, suntan lotion

feel—sandsounds—birds, children, ocean waves

taste—salt water tastes bad

Writing focus: Combining sentences containing adjectives

8 Look at the picture. With a partner, brainstorm a list of adjectives to describe the scene.

9 Read the following paragraphs. How are they the same? How are they different? Which paragraph seems better to you? Explain your choice to a partner. Then check your ideas below.

<table>
<tr><td>

My Mother's Kitchen

1. My mother's kitchen is not big.
2. It is comfortable. 3. It is warm.
4. My mother cooks a lot. 5. Her kitchen smells spicy. 6. It smells sweet.
7. Sometimes she taught my brother and me how to cook. 8. We liked learning new things. 9. We liked working together.
10. We liked making delicious foods.
11. Now I live far away. 12. I often think about my mother's kitchen.

</td><td>

My Mother's Kitchen

1. My mother's kitchen is not big, but it is warm and comfortable. 2. My mother cooks a lot, and her kitchen smells spicy and sweet.
3. Sometimes she taught my brother and me how to cook. 4. We liked learning new things, working together, and making delicious foods.
5. Now I live far away, but I often think about my mother's kitchen.

</td></tr>
</table>

The first paragraph is less interesting because many sentences are all the same type: noun + verb + adjective.

You remember from Unit 2 that sentences about similar topics can often be combined. One effective way to do this is by combining sentences with adjectives.

To make more varied and interesting sentences, you can:

- combine the adjectives in two sentences with *and* or *but*. Remove the subject and verb from the second sentence.

   Example: *The movie was long. The movie was boring.*

   and

   The movie was long. ~~The movie was~~ boring.

   The movie was long and boring.

   Example: *Our homework is difficult. Our homework is fun to do.*

   , but

   Our homework is difficult. ~~Our homework is~~ fun to do.

   Our homework is difficult, but fun to do.

- combine three sentences. Notice how commas are used after the first two adjectives. Remove the subjects and verbs from the second and third sentences.

   Example: *Her skirt was short. It was black. It was fashionable.*

   ,   , and

   Her skirt was short. ~~It was~~ black. ~~It was~~ fashionable.

   Her skirt was short, black, and fashionable.

10 Find and underline three examples of combined sentences in the paragraph on page 20, *Relaxing at the Beach*.

11 Combine these sentences. Then compare with a partner. Which sentences did you combine the same way? Which were different?

   a. Charles is interesting. He is a little strange.

   ....

   b. The river was deep. The river was wide. It was cold.

   ....

   c. Our teacher is strict. He is fair.

   ....

   d. July was hot. It was humid.

   ....

   e. Kim is my best friend because she is kind. She is smart. She is funny.

   ....

   f. The food in that restaurant is delicious. It is expensive.

   ....

Put it together

a Work with a partner to complete the paragraph below and make it better. First, make a list of details you could add to the paragraph. This is an imaginary place, so use your imagination!

A Horrible Hotel

....

The rooms are small. The rooms are dark. The rooms are dirty. There is no air-conditioning. The rooms are hot in summer. There is no heating. The rooms are cold in winter. There are big windows. The view is terrible. ....

....

....

....

That is why I want to warn you never to stay in that hotel.

b On a separate sheet of paper, write your completed paragraph.

- Combine sentences to make it more interesting.
- Write a topic sentence.

c Check your writing.

Did you ...

☐ include a heading on your paper?
☐ format the paragraph properly (see page 2)?
☐ start and end each sentence correctly?

d Exchange papers with another pair. Compare your paragraphs. What is the same? What is different?

e Hand in your paragraph to your teacher.

4 An Exceptional Person

In this unit you will ...
- ■ use word maps to brainstorm.
- ■ practice using adjectives in sentences.
- ■ learn to write concluding sentences.
- ■ learn when to use capital letters.
- ■ write about people.

1 Look at the people and describe them to a partner.

2 Read this paragraph about Jack Collins. Decide which person is most like Jack. Then answer the questions on page 27.

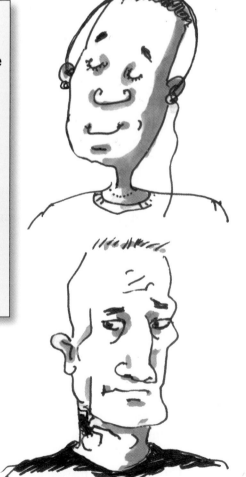

> ### Jack Collins
>
> 1. Jack Collins is the most amazing person I have ever met. 2. He came to my school and talked about his difficult life in prison. 3. He was in prison for 15 years. 4. He made a lot of mistakes when he was young, but now he has changed his life. 5. He saw a lot of violence in prison, so he uses his experience to help high school students. 6. Jack is tall and strong. 7. He also looks a little scary because he has some spider tattoos. 8. The thing I remember most is his sensitive personality. 9. He really wants to help young people. 10. I've never met anyone like Jack before.

a. Which sentence is the topic sentence?

   Circle the topic and underline the main idea.

b. Which sentences tell about Jack's personality?

c. Which sentences tell about Jack's physical appearance?

3 **Find the nouns these adjectives describe:**

a. amazing *person*..........   d. tall, strong ....

b. difficult ....   e. scary   ....

c. young   ....   f. sensitive   ....

> **Note:** Nouns can be used as adjectives; for example, **spider** *tattoos* in the paragraph on page 26 about Jack Collins.

4 **Look again at the paragraph on page 26, *Jack Collins*, and underline the other noun that has been used as an adjective.**

Brainstorming: Word maps

Remember: In Unit 3, you learned that brainstorming was used ...
   - to think of many ideas for your writing.
   - to help you see the connections between ideas.
   and you learned how to brainstorm using lists.

A word map is another kind of brainstorming. Word maps can help you think of many ideas for your writing and see the connections between the ideas.

- Use a separate, whole sheet of paper.
- Write your topic in the middle, and draw a circle around it.
- Write an idea about the topic nearby, and circle it.
- Draw a line to connect the circles. This shows that the idea and the topic are related.
- Add more ideas and circle the ideas.
- Draw lines to connect any circles with related ideas.
- Write down as many ideas as you can. Don't worry about whether they are "good" or "bad."
- After you finish, cross out any ideas you don't want to use.

This example shows a word map for the paragraph on page 26, *Jack Collins*. Notice which ideas the writer kept and which ones he / she crossed out.

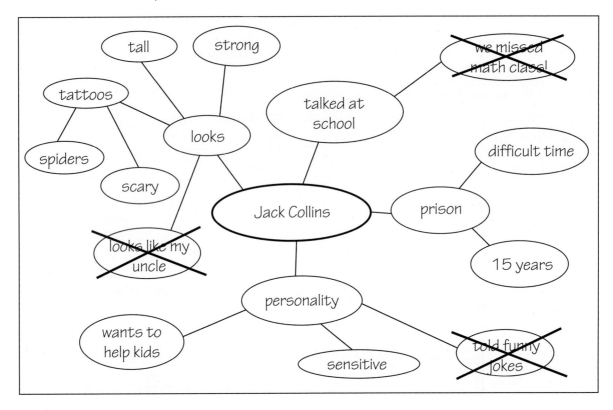

5 **On a separate sheet of paper, make a word map for one of the topics below.**

- Use plenty of descriptive adjectives.
- Share your word map with a partner.
- How many descriptive adjectives did your partner use?

a. A relative

b. A teacher who helped me

c. A movie / music star

Language focus: Using adjectives in sentences

Adjectives can be used in three different ways:

- before a noun
  *Jack Collins is the most **amazing person** I have ever met.*
- after a form of the *be* verb
  *He made a lot of mistakes when **he was young**.*
- after a verb like *taste, sound, look, feel, smell, seem*
  *He also **looks a little scary**.*

6 **Write sentences with each descriptive adjective that you used in your word map. Try to write all three different types of sentence.**

7 **Look at the pictures and do the following.**

a. Write two or three adjectives for each person on a separate sheet of paper. You can write adjectives for their physical appearance or their personality (use your imagination!).

b. Exchange papers with a partner. Write sentences using your partner's adjectives. Then share your sentences.

Writing focus: Concluding sentences

A good paragraph has a clear topic sentence and supporting sentences that explain and support the topic sentence. Many (but not all) paragraphs also have a concluding sentence. The concluding sentence closes the paragraph.

A concluding sentence can ...

- restate the topic sentence.
- summarize the main idea of the paragraph.
- make a prediction connected to the paragraph's topic.
- make a suggestion or give advice connected to the topic.

A concluding sentence **does not** state a completely new idea.

8 Read these concluding sentences for the paragraph on page 26, *Jack Collins*, and decide if they 1 (restate), 2 (summarize), 3 (predict) or 4 (suggest or advise).

a. .... I've never met anyone like Jack before.

b. .... I think Jack will help many teenagers stay out of prison.

c. .... Everyone should talk to someone who has been to prison.

d. .... Jack's experiences, appearance, and personality make him very memorable.

9 The paragraph below is called *My Best Friend's Grandfather*. With a partner, think of three or four things the paragraph could be about.

10 Read the paragraph and find out if any of your guesses were correct.

My Best Friend's Grandfather

1. We can all learn from listening to our grandparents. 2. My best friend's grandfather tells great stories about his life. 3. He's 94 years old, but his voice is still strong and clear. 4. He speaks quietly and slowly when he tells stories. 5. His life was difficult when he was young. 6. His family didn't have much money, and he worked hard. 7. Even though his life was not easy, he is positive and optimistic. 8. I can learn many things from his stories.

....

....

....

---

11 Read the sentences below and do the following.

a. Decide which sentence could not be a concluding sentence for the paragraph *My Best Friend's Grandfather*.

b. Copy the sentence you like best into the paragraph.

c. Tell a partner which concluding sentence you chose and why.

1. My best friend's grandfather is a wonderful storyteller.

2. My best friend's grandfather is a good example for me.

3. My best friend's grandfather never went to college.

4. I think all teenagers should listen to their grandparents' stories.

12 Look at the picture of the soccer player, Iker Casillas, and describe him to a partner.

13 Write a concluding sentence for the paragraph, *A Popular Athlete*, about Iker Casillas. Share your sentence with other students. Decide whether the sentences restate, summarize, predict, or suggest / advise.

A Popular Athlete

Iker Casillas is a famous soccer player from Spain. He is a goalkeeper and also the team captain for the Spanish national team and the club team Real Madrid. He became famous when he was just a teenager, and is now known as one of Europe's best goalkeepers. Casillas is not only a talented player but also a fantastic leader. As team captain, he helped the Spanish national team win their first European Championship in 44 years. In 2010, he led Spain to win their first World Cup ever in an overtime match against the Netherlands. His fans respect him because he is a very hard worker on the field and on the training ground.

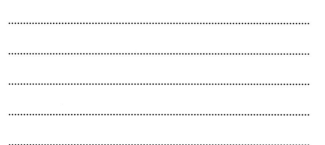

....

....

....

....

....

Language focus: Punctuation

⊃ Capitalization

Remember: In Unit 1, you learned that the first word of a sentence starts with a capital letter.

A word is also capitalized if it is ...

- in the title of a piece of writing (paragraph, essay, book), a movie, a piece of music, etc. Don't capitalize prepositions (*of, to, with*), articles (*a, the*), or conjunctions (*and, but*).
- a name of a group, a place, or a person; that is, a *proper noun*.
- a day of the week or a month.
- a language or a nationality.

> **Note:** A *proper noun* is the name of a specific person, place, or thing. For example, *Picasso* is the name of a specific person, *Paris* is the name of a specific place, *the Olympics* is the name of a specific thing.

14 **Find all of the capitalized words in the paragraph on page 31, *A Popular Athlete*. Tell a partner why each word is capitalized.**

15 **Rewrite the following sentences using correct capitalization.**

   a. iker, whose full name is iker casillas fernandez, was born on may 20, 1981.

   ....

   b. his father, who worked for the ministry of education, and his mother, a hairdresser, both moved from the town of avila to madrid.

   ....

   c. iker is also known for his work with the children's charity organization known as plan.

   ....

   d. in 2009, iker traveled with plan to mali, where he sponsors a child named bourama.

   ....

   e. after the spanish team won the world cup in 2010, children from peru, indonesia, bangladesh, and senegal sent videos to iker to say "congratulations" and to demonstrate their soccer skills.

   ....

   f. his sponsored child bourama said, "iker casillas can teach me how to play when I grow up, and I'll make wonders just like him."

   ....

Put it together

a   With a partner, match the topic sentence on the left to the concluding sentence on the right.

a.	I admire many things about my father.	**1.** You can easily see that he is friendly, outgoing, and loves to laugh.
b.	I think my uncle's face shows his personality.	**2.** She works hard at her job, but she always has time for me.
c.	Daniel Radcliffe, who plays Harry Potter, is my favorite actor.	**3.** His poor health is probably why he died young.
d.	I was always frightened of my history professor.	**4.** When I grow up, I hope I will be just like my father.
e.	My mother is a very busy person.	**5.** She was scary, but I learned a lot from her tough lessons and strict personality!
f.	Elvis' body and health changed as he got older.	**6.** I think he will keep improving as he gets older and makes more movies.

b   Choose one of the pairs of sentences in exercise a above. Make a word map about the topic. Use your imagination!

c   Look at a partner's map and say which ideas are most interesting to you.

d   On a separate sheet of paper, write a paragraph.
- Copy the topic sentence and concluding sentence.
- Add supporting sentences by using the details from your word map.

e   Check your writing.
Did you ...
- ☐ include a heading on your paper?
- ☐ format the paragraph correctly?
- ☐ start and end each sentence correctly?
- ☐ give the paragraph a title?

f   Exchange papers with a partner. Talk with your partner and decide if all the supporting sentences are related to the idea in the topic sentence.

g   Hand in your paragraph to your teacher.

5 Trends and Fads

In this unit, you will ...

■ review descriptive vocabulary.

■ use freewriting to brainstorm.

■ review what a paragraph contains.

■ develop peer feedback skills.

■ write a paragraph about a trend.

I Talk with a partner or small group. In many Western countries, it has become popular for young people to get multiple piercings for their ears. Is this true in your country? Do you know anyone with multiple piercings? Would you ever get them?

2 Why do people get multiple piercings for their ears? With your group or partner, make a list of all the reasons you can think of. Then read this paragraph to see if any of your reasons were mentioned.

A Special Look

1. My best friend thinks I'm crazy. 2. My father is sure I'll regret my decision, and my mother says I've been tricked by a fashion fad. 3. However, I'm glad I got multiple piercings for my ears. 4. I got the idea from a photo in a magazine of a top model. 5. She had a row of diamond studs in each ear, and it looked very elegant. 6. I like being able to wear several earrings at the same time. 7. It's a way for me to express my personality. 8. I know that some people don't think that multiple piercings are attractive, but I am very pleased with this special look.

---

3 Read the paragraph on page 34, *A Special Look,* again and answer the questions.

a. Which sentence is the topic sentence?

1 ☐ 2 ☐ 3 ☐ 4 ☐

b. What do sentences 6 and 7 do?

1. Say the same information in a different way.

2. Tell a story about the topic.

3. Explain the topic sentence by giving more information.

c. Which of these sentences could be added to the paragraph?

1. I buy most of my earrings online.

2. I like looking just a bit different from all of my friends.

3. I know another girl who also has multiple piercings.

4. My parents don't like piercings at all.

Language focus: Vocabulary review

4 Work with a partner. Look at these adjectives from Units 1–4. Do they describe people, places, or things? Write the words in the appropriate column. You can use some words in more than one column. Then add two more words of your own to each column.

busy · convenient · comfortable · common
difficult · exciting · fashionable · friendly
humid · noisy · peaceful · perfect
popular · optimistic · salty · shy
spicy · strong · useful · valuable

people	places	things

Brainstorming: Freewriting

Freewriting is a kind of brainstorming where you write everything you can think of, quickly and without stopping. Freewriting helps to improve your writing fluency, and gives you ideas for your writing.

- Write as much as possible for five or ten minutes.
- Don't worry about spelling, grammar, or punctuation.
- If you make a mistake, just cross it out and continue writing.
- Write continuously, without stopping.

Remember that when you make a list or a word map, you write words or short phrases. When you freewrite, you write sentences.

Look at this example of freewriting on the topic of trends and fashions.

> What is trendy or fashionable now? I can't think of anything. Do I have anything that is fashionable? I don't think so. Everyone has a smart phone now. But smart phones aren't very interesting. What is popular these days? What about ~~televiss~~ TV? Talent shows are popular these days. There are a lot of talent shows on TV these days. With celebrities. "Britain's Next Top Model" is pretty good. I only saw part of last season though because I was out of the country, so I missed the end. I read about it online. But it's better to watch it on TV. Some of those people are really talented, but then some are just dumb. The judges are really funny sometimes. And sometimes they're kind of mean. My roommate likes that show where celebrities compete in a dance contest with real dancers. I forget the name. I saw it a few times, but dancing is boring to me. I can't dance like that. ~~Fashun Fasion~~ Fashion is interesting to me. Modeling is hard, too. It's not an easy job like some people think. A TV show like that is good because it gives some people a chance. Usually only ~~fame~~ famous people or rich people get chances, but this show is for anybody with talent.

5 Choose one of these topics. For five minutes, write as much as you can on a separate sheet of paper. Write everything that comes into your mind, without stopping.

  a. A clothing trend

  b. A fad I don't like

  c. A popular item I own (or would like to own!)

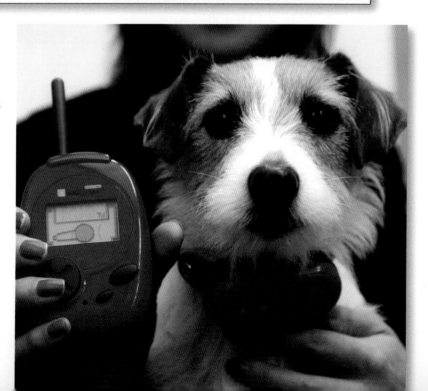

↻ Editing your freewriting

After you freewrite, you need to edit what you have written—go back and see which ideas you can use. It is useful to:

• underline the good ideas.

• cross out anything you don't want to use.

6 Look at the edited freewriting below. What topic do you think the writer will use for his / her paragraph? Why did the writer cross out or underline some sentences? Explain to a partner. Use reasons like these:

• The sentence wasn't about the topic.

• The sentence wasn't interesting.

• The sentence was interesting.

> What is trendy or fashionable now? ~~I can't think of anything. Do I have anything that is fashionable? I don't think so. Everyone has a smart phone now. But smart phones aren't very interesting. What is popular these days? What about televiss TV?~~ Talent shows are popular these days. There are a lot of talent shows on TV these days. With celebrities. "Britain's Next Top Model" is pretty good. I only saw part of last season though because I was out of the country, so I missed the end. I read about it online. But it's better to watch it on TV. <u>Some of those people are really talented, but then some are just dumb. The judges are really funny sometimes. And sometimes they're kind of mean.</u> ~~My roommate likes that show where celebrities compete in a dance contest with real dancers. I forget the name. I saw it a few times, but dancing is boring to me. I can't dance like that.~~ Fashun Fasion Fashion is interesting to me. Modeling is hard, too. It's not an easy job like some people think. <u>A TV show like that is good because it gives some people a chance. Usually only ~~fame~~ famous people or rich people get chances, but this show is for anybody with talent.</u>

7 Look at your freewriting from exercise 5 on page 36. Underline sentences that you think are interesting or useful. Cross out anything that is not useful.

8 Spend another five minutes freewriting, starting with a sentence or phrase you have underlined.

9 Look at your two examples of freewriting together. Do you have enough ideas for a paragraph? If not, freewrite some more!

Paragraph review

Remember: A paragraph can contain three different types of sentence:
- A **topic sentence**—tells the reader the topic and main idea of the paragraph.
- **Supporting sentences**—develop, explain, and give details about the main idea.
- A **concluding sentence**—restates the topic sentence, summarizes the paragraph, makes a prediction, or gives advice or suggestions.

10 **Below are sentences from a paragraph in the wrong order. Decide if the sentences are topic sentences (T), supporting sentences (S), or concluding sentences (C).**

a. .... So, I bought a bike last week for $250 in a second hand bike sale.

b. .... The colors are bright red, white, and dark blue.

c. .... It's a great bike, and I'm going to have a lot of fun on it.

d. .... Mountain bikes are really popular where I live. Everybody has one.

e. .... The bike is one year old but looks new.

f. .... It looks like a bike you can ride on very rough mountains and over rocks.

11 **Put the sentences above in a logical order. Then write the sentences into a paragraph on a separate sheet of paper. Give the paragraph a title.**

Writing focus: Writing the paragraph

After you have chosen a topic and brainstormed ideas, it is time to write your paragraph.

- a topic sentence first.
- Then write the supporting sentences.
- Finish with a concluding sentence.
- Give your paragraph a title.

But this is only the beginning! Good writers follow three steps to improve their writing. They ...

1. check their work.

2. show their work to someone else.

3. make any necessary additions and changes.

These steps can be repeated several times.

12 With a partner, describe the diagram below. What is happening in each circle?

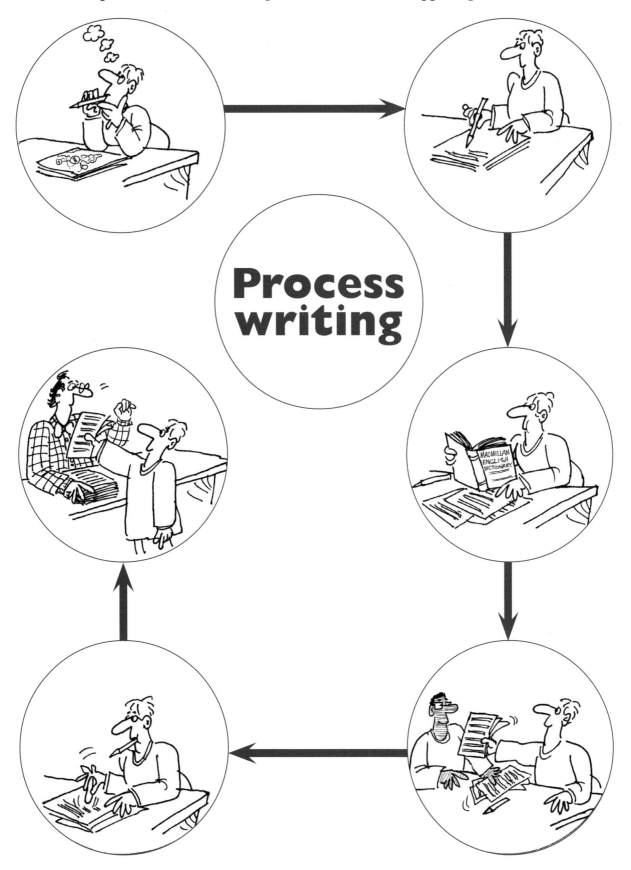

Writing focus: Peer reviewing

Exchanging papers with a classmate, reading each other's paper, and making comments is called *peer reviewing*. When you read a classmate's paper, you can ...

- practice finding topic sentences, supporting sentences, and concluding sentences.

- notice special vocabulary or grammar.

- see different ways to do the same assignment.

- help the writer by saying what ideas you liked best.

- ask questions to help the writer think of more ideas.

- ask a question if you don't understand something—and maybe the writer will think of a better way to explain.

Many writers—even very good writers—feel nervous or shy about sharing their writing. When you write comments about someone's writing, be kind, useful, and truthful. Remember always to say what you like. Comment on ideas and organization, and not spelling or grammar.

13 **With a partner or group, look at the comments below. Put a check (✓) by the ones that are useful for the writer. Put a cross (✗) by the ones that you think aren't useful and give a reason; for example:**

- It isn't kind.

- It isn't clear.

- It isn't useful.

- It (probably) isn't true.

a. ☐ The topic sentence was really interesting.

b. ☐ You don't have any examples.

c. ☐ You have one good example. But your paragraph is a little short. Can you write another example?

d. ☐ I liked your paragraph because it was honest. I think you should add a title.

e. ☐ Your topic sentence and concluding sentence are exactly the same. Maybe one should be different.

f. ☐ I think it's OK.

g. ☐ Your paragraph is not very good. I couldn't understand anything.

h. ☐ Your concluding sentence was funny. I liked it a lot!

i. ☐ You used some interesting vocabulary. It was easy for me to imagine that place.

j. ☐ You are a better writer than Shakespeare!

k. ☐ I'm not sure which sentence is the topic sentence. Is it the first one or the second one? Please tell me.

Put it together

a Use the ideas from your brainstorming from exercises 5 and 8 on pages 36 and 37 to write a paragraph. Write a topic sentence and supporting sentences. Decide if you want to write a concluding sentence.

b Check your writing.

Did you ...

- ☐ include a heading on your paper?
- ☐ format the paragraph properly?
- ☐ start and end each sentence correctly?
- ☐ use capitalization correctly?
- ☐ give the paragraph a title?
- ☐ write a topic sentence?
- ☐ write supporting sentences? How many?
- ☐ use descriptive adjectives?
- ☐ only include one clear idea in each sentence?
- ☐ order the sentences logically?
- ☐ combine sentences logically?
- ☐ write a concluding sentence?

c Exchange papers with a partner. Include your brainstorming.

- Fill out the Peer Review Form on page 92.
- Talk with your partner and go over each form.

d Read your paragraph again.

- Think about the comments from your partner.
- Make any additions or changes to your paragraph that would make it stronger or more interesting.

e Hand in the second draft of your paragraph to your teacher.

6 White Lies

In this unit, you will ...

■ identify opinions and examples in supporting sentences.

■ use discussion to brainstorm.

■ write a paragraph about your opinions.

1 **What is a *white lie*?**

a. A mistake about colors, e.g., "Tom's new car is red" when it is actually purple.

b. A small or unimportant lie you tell not to hurt someone's feelings, e.g., "I think your new car looks cool" when you actually think the new car looks ugly.

c. A type of lie politicians tell to be popular, e.g., "When I am President, everyone will be able to buy a new car" when the politician knows people will not have more money.

• Tell a partner about the last time you told a white lie to a friend, a family member or a teacher.

• Tell your partner if you think it is OK to tell white lies.

2 **Now read this paragraph to find out if the writer agrees with you about telling white lies.**

> ### White Lies
>
> ¹· White lies are not always bad. ²· If you tell your girlfriend that her new haircut looks great when it is horrible, she will know you are lying. ³· I think it is better to tell the truth in this case. ⁴· However, if your girlfriend has a new dress and she really likes it, you should always say it is lovely. ⁵· If you say you don't like it, you will make her unhappy and angry with you. ⁶· You can lie if the truth will hurt and it is not important.

3 **Read the paragraph on page 42, *White Lies*, again and answer these questions.**

  a. Which sentence is the topic sentence?

  b. What does the concluding sentence do?

  1. It restates the topic sentence.

  2. It makes a prediction.

  3. It makes a suggestion.

  c. What do sentences 2 and 4 do?

  1. They give advice.

  2. They give examples.

  3. They tell a story.

Language focus: Giving an opinion

Your *opinion* is your personal feeling. A *fact* is something that is true. Most writing uses both facts and opinions. When you talk about your opinions, you can start your sentence with phrases such as:

I think *friends should always be honest.*

I don't think *white lies are dangerous.*

I believe *it is better to upset your friends than to lie.*

In my view, *it is often safer to lie than to tell the truth.*

In my opinion, *lying is the same as cheating or stealing.*

When you write, you can use one of the sentence starters above. However, be careful not to use too many, or to use them too often. That can make your writing sound weak. The reader knows that the paragraph is your opinion, because you wrote it!

4 **Look at the sentences below. Write F for the facts, and O for the opinions.**

  a. ......*O*. Learning English is easier for girls than for boys.

  ......*F*. There are more boys than girls in my English class.

  b. .... Good teachers don't give too much homework.

  .... Our teacher gave us homework last week.

  c. .... Keanu Reeves is a good actor.

  .... Keanu Reeves starred in the *Matrix* movies.

  d. .... Many teens carry cell phones these days.

  .... Cell phones are very convenient.

  e. .... All students have to wear a uniform at my school.

  .... Our school uniforms are not very comfortable.

  f. .... I don't believe that wearing the latest fashions is important.

  .... My favorite clothes are all black.

5 **For each topic below, write one fact and one opinion.**

- Read your sentences to a partner.
- partner will tell you which sentence is the fact and which is the opinion.

a. tea

Green tea is good for your health.   F

Black tea tastes better than green tea.   O

b. college entrance exams

....

....

c. violent video games

....

....

d. environmental issues

....

....

e. money

....

....

f. sports

....

....

g. (your choice of topic)

....

....

44 WHITE LIES

Brainstorming: Discussion

Talking with other people is a good way to brainstorm:

- You can share ideas with different people.

- You can ask questions to help other students think more deeply.

- When other students ask you questions, you will think of examples to support your opinions.

When you're discussing, it's OK to disagree with your classmates. However, it is important to be respectful of opinions that are different from yours.

6 **Work in a group. Choose two of the topics below, and brainstorm opinions.**

- Think of as many opinions as you can. You don't have to believe them.

- Someone in your group should write down all the opinions in your group.

- Share your opinions with another group or with the whole class.

a. International marriages

b. Truth and lies

c. Playing video games

d. Cheating in school

Writing focus: Supporting sentences with opinions and examples

In your topic sentence and supporting sentences, you can give an opinion. To support your opinion, you could give *examples*, which can either be facts or experiences you've had.

7 **Look again at the paragraph on page 42, *White Lies*. Which sentences are opinions? Which sentences are examples? Are some sentences both?**

8 **Decide if these sentences are opinions (O) or examples (E). Write O or E next to each sentence.**

a. .... Smoking should be banned in all restaurants.

b. .... Smoking is banned in restaurants in California and New York.

c. .... The air is cleaner and healthier in non-smoking restaurants.

d. .... I believe that customers prefer non-smoking restaurants.

e. .... My clothes smelled horrible after I had dinner with a friend who smoked.

f. .... I went to a smoky restaurant in Paris, and I couldn't eat my food.

g. .... In my country, smoking is banned on buses and trains, and in all public buildings.

9 **Read this paragraph and answer the questions below.**

Lying

[1] In my opinion, exaggeration is the same as lying. [2] My friend John is always exaggerating. [3] When we met two years ago, he told me he spoke French fluently. [4] However, last week we met a French man at a soccer match. [5] John couldn't say anything to him in French except, "Where are you from?" and "Do you like England?" [6] I think he lies because he wants to be exciting. [7] Last night, he told me he has a new millionaire girlfriend. [8] She probably has a lot of money but isn't a millionaire. [9] I don't believe John is a good friend.

---

a. Check (✓) the writer's opinions.

1. ☐ A good friend doesn't exaggerate.

2. ☐ A good friend has a rich girlfriend.

3. ☐ A good friend is exciting.

4. ☐ A good friend tells the truth.

b. Underline two examples used to support the writer's opinions.

c. Work with a partner.

1. Give an example of a time you have told a white lie or exaggerated.

2. Tell your partner your opinion about white lies and exaggeration.

Put it together

a **Choose one of the opinions you wrote for exercise 6 on page 45.**

  • Use this opinion for your topic sentence.

  • Brainstorm ideas by discussing the opinion with a small group.

  • Write down examples (facts or experiences) to support your opinion.

b **Write a paragraph. Use opinions and examples.**

c **Check your writing.**

Did you ...

☐ include a heading on your paper?

☐ format the paragraph properly?

☐ start and end each sentence correctly?

☐ use capitalization correctly?

☐ give the paragraph a title?

☐ write a topic sentence?

☐ write supporting sentences? How many?

☐ only include one clear idea in each sentence?

☐ order the sentences logically?

☐ combine the sentences logically?

☐ write a concluding sentence?

d **Exchange papers with a partner.**

  • Fill out the Peer Review Form on page 93.

  • Talk with your partner and go over each form.

e **Read your paragraph again.**

  • Think about the comments from your partner.

  • Make any additions or changes to your paragraph that would make it stronger or more interesting.

f **Hand in the second draft of your paragraph to your teacher.**

7 Explanations and Excuses

In this unit, you will ...

■ develop paragraphs which explain cause and effect / result.

■ combine sentences with *so* and *because*.

■ practice further with word maps and freewriting.

■ write a paragraph about explanations and excuses.

1 Describe this picture to a partner. Guess what the problem is. Tell your partner what you think the people are saying.

2 Read the paragraph and check your guess.

> ### It Wasn't My Fault!
>
> [1] Professors should be understanding when students can't complete assignments on time. [2] I couldn't do the writing homework for English class today, and my professor didn't want to hear my reasons. [3] I had good reasons, too. [4] Last night was Evan's birthday. [5] He's my best friend, so I had to go to his party. [6] After the party, I tried to do the homework, but my computer froze and I lost all the information. [7] I was too tired to write it again because it was very late. [8] My professor didn't care. [9] She said, "You had two weeks to do the assignment, so there are no excuses." [10] I think she's angry with me, but it wasn't my fault.

3 Why didn't the writer do his homework? Write W for the writer's reasons and P for the professor's reasons.

The writer didn't do his homework because ...

a. .... it was his best friend's birthday.

b. .... he is lazy.

c. .... he isn't organized.

d. .... he had a computer problem.

e. .... he isn't a serious student.

Language focus: Giving explanations

Cause and effect / result

- *So* and *because* can be used to join two sentences together:

It was raining. I took an umbrella.

*It was raining, **so** I took an umbrella.*

*I took an umbrella **because** it was raining.*

- *So* and *because* have a similar function.

So tells us the result or effect of a situation:

I took an umbrella.

Because tells us why something happens (the cause):

I took an umbrella. Why? Because it was raining.

- *So* and *because* are often very close in meaning, and you can choose either—but you must use *so* with the result / effect and *because* with the cause:

I had a cold. I didn't go to class.

*I had a cold, **so** I didn't go to class.*

*I didn't go to class **because** I had a cold.*

Note: A comma comes before *so*. There is no comma before *because*.

4 Look again at the paragraph on page 48, *It Wasn't My Fault*, and do the following.

a. Underline the sentences that use *so* or *because*.

b. For each of those sentences, tell a partner what part of the sentence tells the *cause* and what part tells the *effect / result*.

5 Write a sentence using *so* and another sentence using *because* for these situations.

  a. The movie was boring. I left early.

  *The movie was boring, **so** I left early.*

  *I left early **because** the movie was boring.*

  b. We played badly. We lost the soccer match.

  ....

  ....

  c. I failed the test. I didn't study hard.

  ....

  ....

  d. My alarm clock didn't work. I was late for the meeting.

  ....

  ....

  e. I am shy. I don't have many friends.

  ....

  ....

  f. I won't go to the party. I'm tired.

  ....

  ....

Language focus: Starting with because

Look at these two sentences:

*I was too tired to write it again **because** it was very late.*

***Because** it was very late, I was too tired to write it again.*

There is no difference in meaning between these two sentences. When you write, use both styles. This will make your writing more varied and more interesting. However, there is a difference in punctuation.

6 **With a partner, find the difference in punctuation. Write the explanation here.**

....

....

....

7 **Rewrite these sentences using *because*.**

a. I couldn't bring my homework. My dog ate my homework.

*I couldn't bring my homework **because** my dog ate it.*...

***Because** my dog ate my homework, I couldn't bring it.*...

b. I am too busy. I don't exercise.

....

....

c. I have too much homework. I go to bed late.

....

....

d. I can't give up smoking. I will put on weight.

....

....

e. I lost my friend's book. I was careless.

....

....

f. I'm not going to go to the beach. I have to take an exam.

....

....

Brainstorming: Practice with word maps and freewriting

8 Look at this word map and answer the questions below.

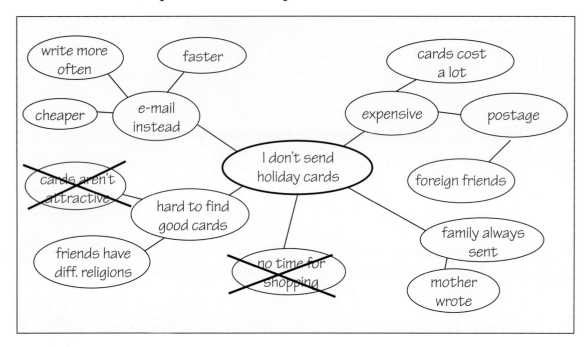

a. What is the writer's topic?

b. How many examples does the writer have?

c. Why did the writer cross out some ideas?

9 Read this paragraph. Were your guesses from exercise 8 above correct? Look at the word map again, and write a topic sentence for the paragraph. Then complete the paragraph with *so* or *because*.

Why I Don't Send Holiday Cards

My family has always sent holiday cards to friends. ....

....

One reason is that I have friends all over the world, [a.] .... sending cards to them would be expensive. In addition, it's difficult to choose the right cards [b.] .... my friends have different religious beliefs. Finally, I e-mail my friends almost every week. [c.] .... I contact them so often, I don't have anything special to say at holiday times. Even though I don't send holiday cards, I am still close to my friends.

10 Look at this picture, and think about what is happening.

11 Freewrite for five minutes about how the driver explains the cause of the accident.

Remember: When you are freewriting, ...
- write for five minutes without stopping.
- write as much as you can. You can cross out ideas you don't like later.
- don't worry about spelling, grammar, or organization.

12 Check and edit your freewriting. Using your ideas, write at least three sentences with *so* or *because*. Then share your sentences with a partner or small group.

Put it together

a   Choose one of these topics and make a word map or freewrite to get some ideas.

  a.   A time I was late

  b.   An accident

  c.   A mistake

  d.   It wasn't my fault!

b   Edit your brainstorming. Cross out ideas you don't want to use and add more ideas if necessary.

c   Write a paragraph about your topic and then check your writing.

d   Exchange papers with a partner. Include your brainstorming.

  •   Fill out the Peer Review Form on page 94.

  •   Talk with your partner and go over each form.

e   Read your paragraph again.

  •   Think about the comments from your partner.

  •   Make any additions or changes to your paragraph that would make it stronger or more interesting.

f   Hand in the second draft of your paragraph to your teacher.

8 Problems and Challenges

In this unit, you will ...

- ▓ express personal feelings about problems.
- ▓ practice using *would like to*, *want to*, and *have to*.
- ▓ learn to order supporting sentences logically.
- ▓ edit lists by ordering ideas logically.
- ▓ write about problems or difficulties.

1 In a small group, describe problems you have with one of the following:

- family and friends
- teachers, classes and studying
- money and budgeting
- expressing your feelings and ideas

2 This paragraph is about a problem with parents. Read the paragraph to see if you share the problem and if you agree with the writer.

Talking to Parents

1. Talking to friends and classmates is easy for a lot of teenage boys, but talking to parents is more difficult. 2. Many teenage boys would like to talk to their fathers about their feelings, but they don't know how. 3. Sons often want to know how their fathers feel about them. 4. For example, I would like my father to say that he is proud of me. 5. However, my father never talks about his feelings. 6. He only wants to talk about sports or my schoolwork. 7. Parents have to talk to their kids about their feelings, or their children will feel lonely at home.

3 **With a partner, answer these questions.**

    a. Which sentence is the topic sentence?

    b. What does the concluding sentence do? (You can check more than one answer.)

        1. ☐ It restates the topic sentence.

        2. ☐ It makes a prediction.

        3. ☐ It makes a suggestion.

        4. ☐ It summarizes the paragraph.

    c. Which of these details and examples could be added to the paragraph on page 55? Explain why the others do not belong.

        1. ☐ My father is 58 years old.

        2. ☐ My father's parents don't talk about their feelings either.

        3. ☐ My father is often busy with his job, so I don't have many chances to see him.

        4. ☐ Many parents like to play tennis and golf on the weekend.

        5. ☐ It's also hard to choose a good birthday gift for my father.

        6. ☐ I guess if I want to talk with my father, I will have to start more conversations myself.

Language focus: Want to, would like to, have to

Want to and *would like to* are useful expressions for talking about wishes:

I **want to** *get a good job.*

Miwa **would like to** *travel overseas.*

> **Note:** In speech and informal writing, the contraction *I'd like to* is often used. However, in academic writing, contractions are less common. Use *I would like to* when you write.

Have to shows *obligation* (that you must do something, or that it is required):

Mei Mei **has to** *get up early to get to school on time.*

If you want to drive a car, you **have to** *get a driver's license.*

4 **Read the paragraph on page 55, *Talking to Parents*, again and underline the sentences containing *want to*, *would like to*, and *have to*.**

5 Complete these sentences with the correct form of *want to*, *would like to*, or *have to*.

a. Kelly .... clean her room. It's a mess!

b. Ji Eun .... take dance lessons, but she doesn't have enough money.

c. Ali and Khalid .... go to the party, but they can't find a ride.

d. I .... go out last night, but I .... work at my part-time job.

e. My parents say if I want a new bicycle, I will .... pay for it myself.

f. If you .... work in Spain, you .... learn Spanish.

g. My little sister is always bothering me when I .... be alone.

6 Complete these sentences. Then share with a partner.

a. I would like ....

b. I have to ....

c. I want to .... , but I have to ....

d. When I was a child, I wanted to ....

e. Last year, I had to ....

f. I wish I didn't have to .... !

Writing focus: Order of supporting ideas

After brainstorming ideas for a paragraph, you need to decide which ideas to use and the order you will write the ideas.

Ideas and sentences need to be ordered logically.

- Sentences that are part of the same idea go together.

- Sentences can go in *chronological* (time) order.

- Sentences can go in order of importance (see explanation below).

One way to organize your supporting sentences is to decide which ideas are most important. Writers often put the most important ideas last in a paragraph, so the strongest sentences are the last ones the reader sees. When you edit ideas in a list, you can number them in order of importance.

> **Remember:** When brainstorming, ...
> - use a separate, whole sheet of paper.
> - collect as many ideas as possible (don't stop writing).
> - don't worry if you don't like the ideas.
> - write short phrases or single words for lists and word maps, and sentences for freewriting.
> - after you brainstorm, look at the relevant ideas and brainstorm again.
> - edit your brainstorming before you write your paragraph.

7 **Look at the list of ideas for a paragraph called *Making Language Classes Interesting*.**

- Number the brainstormed ideas in order of importance (write 1 by the most important idea, 2 by the second most important idea, and so on).

- The writer decided not to use two details from the list. Which were they, and why?

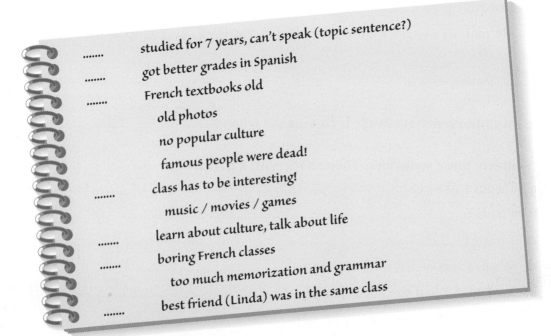

8 Read the paragraph *Making Language Classes Interesting* to see if the writer's order of importance was the same as yours.

> Making Language Classes Interesting
>
> [1.] Learning a language is difficult, but it doesn't have to be boring. [2.] I studied French at school for seven years, but I cannot speak a word of French now. [3.] The problem with learning French was my classes, not the language. [4.] One problem was that our textbooks were too old and boring. [5.] The pictures were black and white, and the famous singers and movie stars had already died! [6.] We also wanted to learn about popular French culture and talk about our lives in French. [7.] Students do not want to memorize rules and vocabulary for an hour everyday and nothing else. [8.] The most important point is that the classroom has to be interesting. [9.] Students need to play games, listen to music, watch movies and talk about them in the foreign language. [10.] Teachers need to make language classes useful and interesting if they want students to learn.

9 Look at these sentences for a paragraph called *The Challenge of Running a Marathon*. Number the sentences in chronological order.

- [1] Last year I ran the New York marathon, and it was the hardest thing I've ever done.
- [ ] The twenty-mile point was the worst because I had been running for three hours, I was hungry, and I was in a lot of pain.
- [ ] The beginning of the race was a lot of fun because the crowd was cheering and the sun was shining.
- [ ] I had to spend about six months training for the marathon before it even started.
- [ ] When I crossed the finish line, I could hardly walk and I felt sick.
- [ ] Next year, I would like to watch the marathon but not run it.
- [ ] After thirteen miles, the middle of the marathon, my legs began to hurt and I started to get bored.
- [ ] On the day of the marathon, I had to get up at 5:00 a.m. and get to the starting line. It was cold, and everyone was very tired.

10 Look at the paragraph *Not Enough Time below* and do the following.

   a. Choose *three* of the supporting ideas below the paragraph.

   b. Write the sentences into the paragraph.

   c. Put the most important example last.

   d. Share your paragraph with a partner.

> **Note:** It's OK to have a different order—but be sure to explain your choices!

Not Enough Time

Should I quit my part-time job? I like my job as a waiter in a Chinese restaurant because the food is good, the atmosphere is friendly, and I can earn some money. But it is causing some problems for me.

Even though I like my job, I might quit until I finish school, or ask my boss if I can work fewer hours.

- The cooks let me test the food sometimes, and I am gaining weight.

- I would like to see my friends more often, but I have to work almost every night.

- It's hard for me to finish my homework. I want to concentrate on my studies, but I am too tired after work.

- I want to be a journalist and I would like to spend my free time writing stories about the people in my town. I can't do this and work so many hours.

- I have to drive to work, and my car is very old. I'm afraid it will wear out because I am driving it too much.

11 Look again at the paragraph on page 60, *Not Enough Time.* Why did the writer begin with a question? Share your ideas with a partner or group.

    a. The writer didn't know some information.

    b. The writer wanted to get some advice from another person.

    c. To make the reader interested in the topic.

    d. The writer didn't understand the topic very well.

Put it together

a Choose one of these topics and then brainstorm the topic by making a list.

    a. A problem with a friend

    b. A problem at school

    c. A problem at work

    d. A problem in your city / school

b Edit your list.

- Cross out ideas you don't want to use and add more ideas if necessary.

- Number the other ideas in order of importance.

- Share your list with a partner, and explain your choices.

c Write a paragraph about your topic and then check your writing.

d Exchange papers with a partner. Include your brainstorming.

- Fill out the Peer Review Form on page 95.

- Talk with your partner and go over each form.

e Read your paragraph again.

- Think about the comments from your partner.

- Make any additions or changes to your paragraph that would make it stronger or more interesting.

f Hand in the second draft of your paragraph to your teacher.

9 Strange Stories

In this unit you will ...
- use time expressions: *after*, *before*, and *when*.
- learn to identify the main parts of a narrative.
- practice ordering the events in a narrative in a logical way.
- write a paragraph about interesting or unusual experiences.

1 Look at the picture. What do you think is happening? Share your ideas with a partner or group. Then read the paragraph below and check your guesses.

A UFO Sighting

1. I never believed in aliens before one night last year. 2. It was a cold, dark winter evening, and I was walking home from a friend's house. 3. I stopped to tie my shoe. 4. When I looked up again, I saw a round object coming toward me. 5. It was very large and shiny. 6. I couldn't believe what I was seeing. 7. Before I could shout or run, the object suddenly moved and then disappeared. 8. After the object disappeared, I ran all the way home and called my best friend. 9. When she picked up the phone, I couldn't say anything. 10. I knew she would think I was crazy. 11. I never told anyone about my UFO sighting.

2 Read the paragraph in exercise 1 above again and answer these questions.
   a. Which sentence is the topic sentence?
   b. How is this paragraph developed?
   - **1.** by telling a story
   - **2.** by giving reasons
   - **3.** by describing objects with details
   c. What does sentence 2 do?
   - **1.** It gives details about the topic sentence.
   - **2.** It tells the reader when and where the event happened.
   - **3.** It lets the reader know the paragraph will talk about UFOs.
   d. Is sentence 11 a concluding sentence?

Language focus: Using time expressions

One way to order two events is to use *after, before,* or *when.*

After shows the first event:

*I played soccer **after school**.* (school happened first; not soccer)

***After school,** I played soccer.*

Before shows the second event:

*I couldn't play the guitar **before I took lessons**.* (lessons happened first)

***Before I took lessons,** I couldn't play the guitar.*

When shows that the first event happened just before the second event:

*I told him the news **when he called**.* (he called first; then I told him the news)

***When he called,** I told him the news.*

> **Note:** When *after, before,* or *when* begin a sentence, use a comma after the event.

3   **Join these ideas with *after, before,* or *when*. Add a comma if necessary.**

a. ....*After*........ the movie, we went home.

d. I left my house .... you called.

b. We left the class .... we turned in our assignments.

e. Please finish your homework .... you watch TV!

c. I woke up .... the alarm clock rang.

f. .... the dog barked, the baby cried.

4 Look at these pictures. What strange thing happened? Share your guesses with a partner.

5 Read the paragraph *Sleeping in a Farmhouse* to see if your guess in exercise 4 above was correct. Then complete the paragraph with *after*, *before*, or *when*.

Sleeping in a Farmhouse

The strangest experience in my life happened a year [a.] .... I graduated from high school. I was sixteen years old and my best friend Mark was fifteen. He invited me to visit him during the summer. I was staying with him in his farmhouse in the middle of the countryside. I shared a room with Mark, and our beds were separated by a table. Every morning, Mark's mom brought us a cup of hot tea in bed [b.] .... we woke up. While we were sleeping one night, I could feel my bed moving. I thought I was dreaming. The next morning, Mark's mother brought us hot tea as usual. [c.] .... she turned on the lights, we saw that our beds were pushed together and the table had moved. Mark said he didn't do it, and I didn't do it. We still don't know how the beds moved! What do you think?

6 With a partner, think of different explanations for why the beds moved. (You can draw a picture of what happened to help explain.) Then share your ideas with another pair or the whole class.

Writing focus: Narrative paragraphs

Narratives tell stories. Everyone has read narratives, watched them on television or at the movies, or heard them from other people. A narrative paragraph tells a short story or describes an event.

The paragraph *Sleeping in a Farmhouse* is a narrative about two boys on vacation. In the story their beds move in the middle of the night, and they don't know how it happened.

The events (stages of the story) are told in a logical order:

1. **Background information**

   A narrative paragraph usually starts with background information to set the scene for the story and provide context. It can tell **when** and **where** a story happened:

   > The strangest experience in my life happened a year before I graduated from high school. I was sixteen years old and my best friend Mark was fifteen. He invited me to visit him during the summer.

2. **Beginning of the story**

   The beginning of a narrative usually tells what happened first in the story:

   > I was staying with him in his farmhouse in the middle of the countryside. I shared a room with Mark, and our beds were separated by a table. Every morning, Mark's mom brought us a cup of hot tea in bed after we woke up.

3. **Middle of the story**

   The middle of the narrative is usually the main part and tells most of the events in the story:

   > While we were sleeping one night, I could feel my bed moving. I thought I was dreaming. The next morning, Mark's mother brought us hot tea as usual. When she turned on the lights, we saw that our beds were pushed together and the table had moved.

4. **End of the story**

   The end of a narrative concludes the story. It tells the final event, and has a concluding remark:

   > Mark said he didn't do it, and I didn't do it. We still don't know how the beds moved! What do you think?

7 Look at these pictures from a story. In a small group, describe what happened.

8 Read these parts of a paragraph about the pictures in exercise 7 above. Decide if the parts are ...

- background information.
- from the beginning of the story.
- from the middle of the story.
- from the end of the story.

Then number the parts in the correct order. (There are two parts of the middle section.)

a. ☐ ....

A few days later my father was able to go to the window to look for himself. But all he could see was an ugly brick wall.

b. ☐ ....

A strange thing happened to my father when he was in the hospital to have an operation.

c. ☐ ....

The next day he asked the nurse why the man described a beautiful park. The nurse looked confused and told my father, "That man was blind."

d. ☐ ....

My father didn't feel well. He asked the other man to describe the view outside the window because he wanted to feel better. After the man talked about the beautiful view from the window, my father was able to fall asleep. Before my father woke up, the man left the hospital.

e. ☐ ....

After his operation, my father woke up sharing a room with another man. The other man's bed was next to the window.

9 Read the parts below of two stories, *A Fright in the Forest* and *A Strange Day in Class*. Number the parts in the correct order and decide if they are ...

- background information.
- from the beginning of the story.
- from the middle of the story.
- from the end of the story.

Note: The middle parts are not complete!

A Fright in the Forest

a. ☐ ....

Suddenly, I felt very cold and scared.

b. ☐ ....

I grew up in a small town in the countryside. Near my house was a large forest, and my parents told me not to play there.

c. ☐ ....

After that day, I never went back to the forest.

d. ☐ ....

One day, I was playing in the forest with some of my school friends.

A Strange Day in Class

a. ☐ ....

I have been studying English for a few years and I really enjoy the classes.

b. ☐ ....

I heard everyone laughing. I woke up and realized it was a dream.

c. ☐ ....

One day something unusual happened in class.

d. ☐ ....

The teacher was explaining grammar when I saw something strange out of the window.

10 With a partner, brainstorm what happened in each story. Then write sentences to complete the middle part of each story. Share your paragraph with another pair or the class.

Remember: Brainstorming ...
- helps you collect ideas.
- helps you be creative and imaginative.
- can be done by discussing ideas.

Put it together

a   Choose one of these topics.

   a. A coincidence

   b. A strange experience

   c. A funny story

b   Choose one of the methods of brainstorming you have practiced, and brainstorm
   the story.

   • making a list

   • making a word map

   • freewriting

   • discussion

c   Edit your brainstorming.

   • Cross out ideas you don't want to use and add more ideas if necessary.

   • Share your brainstorming with a partner, and explain your choices.

d   Write a paragraph about your topic and then check your writing.

e   Exchange papers with a partner. Include your brainstorming.

   • Fill out the Peer Review Form on page 96.

   • Talk with your partner and go over each form.

f   Work with a new partner. Tell him / her about the story that you read in exercise e
   above. Listen to your partner tell someone else's story.

g   Read your paragraph again.

   • Think about the comments from your partner.

   • Make any additions or changes to your paragraph that would make it stronger or
     more interesting.

h   Hand in the second draft of your paragraph to your teacher.

10 Differences

In this unit, you will ...
- use double lists to brainstorm.
- use *whereas* and *however* to make comparisons.
- learn to organize a comparison paragraph.
- compare different situations / events.
- write a paragraph about the changes in your life.

1 Look at the pictures. Tell a partner what you think the differences are between high school and college life for this woman.

2 Read this paragraph and find out the important differences for the writer.

College Life

[1.] My life changed a lot when I was in college. [2.] There were 600 students in my high school and I knew nearly everyone. [3.] However, there were thousands of students in my college, and I didn't know anyone. [4.] I felt very lonely. [5.] In high school, the classes were half boys and half girls. [6.] In college, I studied engineering, and there weren't many women in the classes. [7.] The biggest change in college was the style of class. [8.] We had to do a lot of reading and learning on our own in college, whereas in high school the teacher told us nearly everything to study for the exams. [9.] Even though college was more difficult, I enjoyed it more than my school days—after I got used to it!

---

3 **Read the paragraph on page 69, *College Life*, again and answer these questions with a partner.**

    a. How many differences between high school and college does the writer mention? What are they?

    b. The writer says that the biggest difference between high school and college was the style of class. Do you think this was a positive or negative difference? Explain your opinion to a partner.

    c. What are or what will be the differences for you between high school and college?

Brainstorming: Double lists

4 **Look at the pictures and tell a partner how you think the summer and winter are different in Maine.**

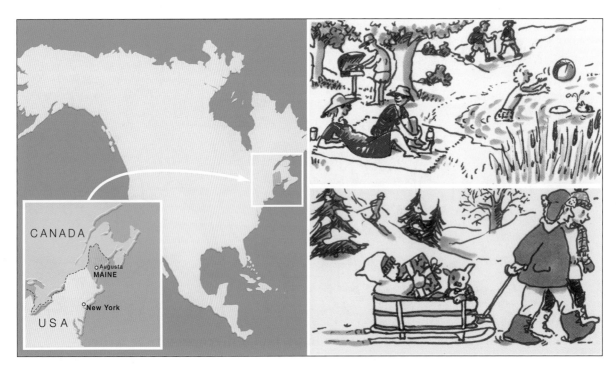

5 **Read this paragraph and decide if the writer prefers the summer or winter in Maine.**

Winter in Maine

1. Spend a year in Maine and you'll be amazed by the difference between the summer and winter seasons. 2. The summer season is hot, and everyone likes to swim in the rivers and have barbeques. 3. People also go on hikes in the many mountains and through the national parks. 4. Summer in Maine is very green, and many tourists visit the countryside. 5. However, the winter is even more spectacular. 6. It snows a lot in Maine in the winter, and the scenery looks beautiful. 7. It sometimes snows two feet in one day, which is great for skiing and snowboarding. 8. The best part about the winter is Christmas. 9. There are a lot of parties in December, and people share Christmas presents or cards with friends, family, classmates, and colleagues.

6 Read the paragraph again and look at this brainstormed list. Underline the ideas the writer used from it.

Summer		Winter	
hot	hiking in mountains / parks	cold	snowboarding / skiing
barbeques	air-conditioning	parties	Christmas parties
shorts / T-Shirts	long, sunny days	scarves / hats / gloves	sharing presents and cards
sunglasses	vacation	snow	short, dark days
swimming in river	my birthday	beautiful scenery	

Note: The writer used a *double list* technique to brainstorm ideas for the paragraph describing differences between summer and winter in Maine. A double list is useful when you are comparing two subjects.

7 Choose one of the topics below. Use a double list to brainstorm ideas.

• Share your list with a partner.

• Discuss which ideas would be good to write about.

a. Elementary school / high school

b. Last year's fashions / this year's fashions

c. My best friend five years ago / my best friend now

d. What was important to me at thirteen years old / what is important now

Language focus: **However / whereas**

However and *whereas* can be used to connect two different or opposite ideas:

my friends prefer watching movies / I find books more interesting

My friends prefer watching movies. **However,** *I find books more interesting.*

My friends prefer watching movies, **whereas** *I find books more interesting.*

Whereas *my friends prefer watching movies, I find books more interesting.*

Note: You can join two sentences with *whereas*. Use *whereas* at the beginning of a sentence or in the middle, after a comma. Use *however* at the beginning of a sentence.

8 Look again at the paragraph on page 69, *College Life* and the paragraph on page 70, *Winter in Maine.* Underline the sentences that use *however* and *whereas*. Note the punctuation used with these words.

9 Connect these ideas with *whereas* or *however*. Add punctuation where needed.

a. (*however*) skiing is a popular winter sport / many young people prefer snowboarding

b. (*whereas* first) my science class has over 300 people in it / my English seminar has just twelve

c. (*whereas* in the middle) dogs are more faithful / cats are more independent

d. (*however*) cars are faster / I'd rather ride my bicycle

e. (*however*) DVDs are more common these days / I have a huge video tape collection

f. (*whereas*) (your ideas)

Writing focus: Organizing a comparison paragraph

When you compare two things (high school life and university life; summer and winter weather), you have two choices for organizing your paragraph:

- You can write all about the first subject and then all about the second (*block style*).

First block about the summer in Maine. ⟶

Second block about the winter in Maine. ⟶

> Winter in Maine
>
> Spend a year in Maine and you'll be amazed by the difference between the summer and winter seasons. The summer season is hot, and everyone likes to swim in the rivers and have barbeques. People also go on hikes in the many mountains and through the national parks. Summer in Maine is very green, and many tourists visit to see the countryside. However, the winter is even more spectacular. It snows a lot in Maine in the winter, and the scenery looks beautiful. It sometimes snows two feet in one day, which is great for skiing and snowboarding. The best part about the winter is Christmas. There are a lot of parties in December, and people share Christmas presents or cards with friends, family, classmates, and colleagues.

- You choose several points of comparison. Compare first one point about the two topics, then compare a second point about the two topics, and so on (*point-by-point style*).

First point about class size. ⟶

Second point about the number of boys and girls. ⟶

Third point about the class style. ⟶

> College Life
>
> My life changed a lot when I was in college. There were 600 students in my high school and I knew nearly everyone. However, there were thousands of students in my college and I didn't know anyone. I felt very lonely. In high school the classes were half boys and half girls. In college I studied engineering and there weren't many women in the classes.
> The biggest change in college was the style of class. We had to do a lot of reading and learning on our own, whereas in high school the teacher told us nearly everything to study for the exams. Even though college was more difficult, I enjoyed my life more than my school days—after I got used to it!

10 **Look at the maps of the UK and Australia.**

    a. In a small group, discuss what you think the differences are between London and Sydney in December.

    b. Make notes of the differences.

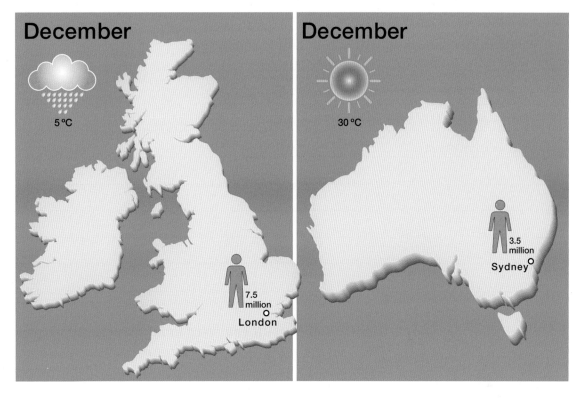

11 **Look at the double list of characteristics of London and Sydney, and add your differences. With a partner, write sentences about the differences using _however_ and _whereas_.**

London	Sydney
in the northern hemisphere	in the southern hemisphere
difficult to make friends	easy to make friends
everyone stayed inside and watched TV	everyone was outside surfing and having barbeques

12 On your own, complete the paragraph below, comparing London with Sydney.

- Using exercises 10 and 11 on page 73, write supporting sentences for the paragraph.
- Remember to arrange the ideas in either block style or point-by-point style.
- Connect at least two ideas with *however* or *whereas*.
- Finish the paragraph with a concluding sentence.

Moving to England

Last December, I moved from Sydney, Australia to London, England with my family, and it was like moving to another planet.

_____

_____

_____

_____

---

13 Share your paragraph with the same group you were in for exercise 10 on page 73.

- How are your paragraphs similar and different?
- Did the others in your group use block style or point-by-point style?

Put it together

a Look at the brainstorming you did for exercise 7 on page 71.

- Edit your brainstorming for a paragraph (or, if you wish, brainstorm again on one of the other topics).
- Decide if you will organize your paragraph in block style or point-by-point style.
- Number your ideas in order of importance.

b Write your paragraph and then check your writing.

c Exchange papers with a partner. Include your brainstorming.

- Fill out the Peer Review Form on page 97.
- Talk with your partner and go over each form.

d Read your paragraph again and make changes to improve it.

e Hand in the second draft of your paragraph to your teacher.

Difficult Decisions

In this unit, you will ...

- practice writing about cause and effect relationships.
- use pair interviews to brainstorm.
- learn how to begin paragraphs with a question.
- write a paragraph about a difficult decision.

1 Talk with a partner or small group. Is it important to keep secrets? Are there any secrets you would tell? Has anyone ever told a secret of yours? Why? How did you feel about it?

> ### Telling a Secret
>
> Do you think it's OK to tell your best friend's secret? Last year, my best friend told me a secret, and she made me promise not to tell anyone. My friend is slim, but she thought she was fat. Consequently, she wouldn't eat any food, and she became anorexic. I didn't know what to do. Because I thought she might get angry, I hesitated to tell her parents or teachers. However, I finally decided to tell her parents. As a result, they made sure my friend ate all her meals. They also took her to a psychologist every week for six months. Because of her parents' and the psychologist's help, my friend is much healthier now. I thought my friend would hate me for telling her parents about her problem, but last week she thanked me. I'm glad I told her secret.

2 Read the paragraph above and discuss with a partner. Which of these events happened first? Write 1 by the first one and 2 by the second.

- **a.** .... My friend thought she was fat. .... My friend wouldn't eat any food.
- **b.** .... I hesitated to tell her parents. .... I thought she might get angry.
- **c.** .... Her parents made sure she ate all her meals. .... I told her parents her secret.
- **d.** .... My friend is healthier now. .... Her parents and the psychologist helped her.

3 Why did the writer start her paragraph with a question?
- **a.** She wanted her readers' opinions about her decision.
- **b.** She needed some information she didn't have.
- **c.** She wanted her readers to think deeply about her topic.
- **d.** She is worried she made the wrong decision.

4 How did the writer develop her paragraph?
- **a.** She gave a lot of examples.
- **b.** She used a narrative.
- **c.** She described her friend carefully.

Language focus: Cause and effect

Remember: In Unit 7, you used *so* and *because* to write about cause and effect.
Because tells us the cause of an action or a situation.
So tells us the effect.

Below are some words and expressions, which, like *so*, show effect.
Use a variety of expressions in your writing to keep it interesting.

As a result, consequently, and *therefore* are all used to connect two ideas. They all have a similar meaning. They show that the second sentence was the effect, or result, of the first one. They can be used at the beginning of the second sentence or they can join the two sentences with the word *and* before them.

as a result

I finally decided to tell her parents. **As a result,** *they made sure my friend ate all her meals.*
I finally decided to tell her parents, and **as a result** *they made sure my friend ate all her meals.*

consequently

My friend thought she was fat. **Consequently,** *she wouldn't eat any food.*
My friend thought she was fat, and **consequently** *she wouldn't eat any food.*

therefore

My friend thought she was fat. **Therefore,** *she wouldn't eat any food.*
My friend thought she was fat, and **therefore** *she wouldn't eat any food.*

5 **Look at the example sentences above.**

    a. If *as a result, consequently,* or *therefore* begin a sentence, where is a comma used?

    b. If they join two sentences with *and*, where is a comma used?

6 **Connect these sentences with *as a result, consequently,* or *therefore*. Think about the correct order of the sentences and use correct punctuation.**

    a. I didn't go to college right away. I wanted to travel for a year after high school.

    b. My parents needed help in their restaurant. I moved back home and worked for them.

    c. Cars are very convenient. People use them more than they should.

    d. My visa wasn't issued in time. I had to change my airplane ticket.

    e. Our school didn't have a lot of money. The administration decided to cancel some after-school clubs.

    f. I joined a social networking site that I don't actually like. My friends complained that it was hard to communicate with me.

Brainstorming: Pair interviews

You have already used discussion for brainstorming in Unit 6. Talking with just one person can also help you think of ideas for writing because that person can ask you focused questions about your topic. Your partner might ask you questions that begin with words like *what, why, how long, when,* and so on.

For example, when the writer of *Telling a Secret* told her partner about her difficult decision, her partner asked her questions such as *When did this happen? How did you find out about her problem? Why didn't you tell her parents immediately? What happened next? How did you feel? Do you think you made the right decision?*

To use pair interviews effectively, follow these steps:

• Tell your partner as much as you can about your topic.

• When you run out of things to say, your partner will ask you questions to help you continue.

• Write down the ideas that you talk about.

You won't use all of the ideas for your paragraph. However, it's always better to have too many ideas and then edit them.

7 **With a partner, look at the pictures of a woman who had to make a difficult decision, and do the following.**

a. Tell your partner what's happening in each picture.

b. Write a list of questions that you could ask the woman about her difficult decision.

c. Share your list of questions with another pair.

8 Read this paragraph. Did the writer answer any of the questions you wrote with your partner?

> ### Studying Abroad
>
> Going to Australia was a difficult decision for me. I wanted to go to Australia to get a degree in Business Administration, but my parents didn't want me to leave home. I knew I would miss my friends and family too, because I would be in Australia for four years. In the end, I decided to study in Australia to improve my career. As a result, I now speak English very well, and I work for a large international company. Because of all the languages I speak, I also travel around the world a lot with my company. Therefore, I don't regret going to Australia.

9 Choose one of these topics. Then work with a partner. Your partner will ask you questions about your topic. Write down your partner's questions. At the end of the exercise, tell your partner which questions were the most helpful (helped you think of the most or the best ideas).

a. Telling a secret / keeping a secret

b. A time I changed my mind

c. Choosing a job

d. Choosing a school / university

e. Starting / stopping an activity

Writing focus: Using questions to catch attention

A question at the beginning of your paragraph can encourage your reader to think deeply about your topic. Questions can be used to start paragraphs about a difficult decision, opinions, or personal feelings. In the opening paragraph in this unit, the writer asked, *Do you think it's OK to tell your best friend's secret?* This question helps the reader to think about the topic of secrets and telling them.

However, questions can be difficult to use effectively. The best questions are ones that help the reader to focus on and think about your topic. You need to imagine your audience (the people who will read your writing) and imagine how they might answer the question.

- Will the answer be too easy or too obvious?

- Could the reader give an answer very different from yours?

If the writer of *Telling a Secret* had asked *Have you ever told your best friend's secret?* or *Have you ever had a friend with anorexia?*, the reader might have answered "No" in his / her mind, and then lost interest in the topic.

If the writer had asked, *Do you know what anorexia is?*, the reader might have answered *Of course!* and thought that the paragraph topic would be too simple.

10 Below are several topics and some questions for the first sentence. Check (✔) the questions that are good. Discuss your choices with a partner.

Studying in Australia

☐ Have you ever been to Australia?
☐ Is it more important to be safe or to follow your dream?
☐ Where do you want to go to college?
☐ Can where you study change your life?

Quitting smoking

☐ Is smoking a choice or a disease?
☐ Do you smoke?
☐ Do you know how to quit smoking?
☐ Is it possible to be completely free of an addiction?

Breaking up with a girlfriend

☐ Do you have a girlfriend?
☐ Do you want to break up with your girlfriend?
☐ Can a former girlfriend really become your friend?
☐ Is there a kind way to tell someone you no longer love her?

Put it together

a Look at the paragraph topics from exercise 9 on page 78, and choose a new one (or choose your own topic about a difficult decision).

b Talk with a partner about your paragraph topic. Write down any good ideas that come from your discussion. If you need more ideas, talk with another partner, or try your favorite method of brainstorming.

c Write your paragraph and then check your writing.

d Exchange papers with a partner.
   • Fill out the Peer Review Form on page 98.
   • Talk with your partner and go over each form.

e Read your paragraph again and make changes to improve it.

f Hand in the second draft of your paragraph to your teacher.

12 *Fate or Choice?*

In this unit you will ...
- write about hopes and plans for the future.
- review brainstorming techniques.
- review connecting words and phrases.
- write a paragraph about the future.

1 Look at the pictures. Tell a partner what is happening. What will happen next?

2 Have you ever bought a lottery ticket or entered a drawing? Why, or why not? Have you ever won? Share your experiences with a group.

3 Read this paragraph to find out if the writer believes in luck.

Do You Believe in Luck?

^{1.} My parents and friends think that buying lottery tickets is foolish. ^{2.} They say that ordinary people like me never win, and that it's just a waste of money. ^{3.} However, I don't agree with this because I know that ordinary people win things. ^{4.} For example, I've entered drawings before, and I've won several times. ^{5.} I won a T-shirt at my school festival once, and also a gift certificate in a department store. ^{6.} In addition, my uncle won a free dinner for two people by putting his business card in a drawing at a restaurant. ^{7.} I hope to win a lot of money in the lottery in the future, so I'm going to buy a few lottery tickets. ^{8.} After all, someone has to win the lottery, and it could be me one day!

---

4 **Look again at the paragraph on page 80, *Do You Believe in Luck?* Then answer these questions with a partner.**

   a. Does the author have the same opinion as you?

   b. Which sentence is the topic sentence?

     1 ☐   2 ☐   3 ☐

   c. Which sentence shows the writer's opinion?

   d. Which sentences support the writer's opinion?

   e. Which sentences conclude the paragraph?

     5 and 6 ☐   6 and 7 ☐   7 and 8 ☐

   f. Underline the sentences where the writer talks about the future.

Language focus: Writing about hopes and plans

To talk about your hopes and plans for the future you can use expressions such as *I would like to, I hope to,* and *I want to.*

I would like to be a journalist.

I hope to get a job in engineering when I finish college.

I want to live a long life, so I never take risks on the road.

Two verb phrases to write about definite plans for the future are *be going to* and *plan to.*

I'm going to buy a few lottery tickets.

I plan to buy a few lottery tickets.

5 **Write sentences expressing each of the following personal wishes or plans. Use a variety of forms.**

   a. Tomas / professional race car driver

   Tomas wants to be a professional race

   car driver.

   b. Sandra / politician

   ....

   c. Cooper / married with children in ten years

   ....

   d. Diana / Olympic medal in 2016

   ....

   e. Andrea / a sports car soon

   ....

   f. Write a sentence about a dream / hope that you have.

   ....

   g. Write a sentence about a plan that you have.

   ....

Brainstorming: Review

6 **Work with a partner and do the following.**

    a. Take turns describing how to do these different types of brainstorming:

        1. list

        2. word map

        3. freewriting

        4. discussion

        5. list showing order of importance

        6. list showing chronological order

        7. double list

        8. pair interview

    b. Explain to your partner which type of brainstorming ...

- is the easiest for you to begin.
- helps you get the most ideas.
- helps you get the most useful ideas.
- is the most difficult for you.
- is your favorite.

7 **Choose two or three of these topics. Do a different type of brainstorming for each topic.**

    a. A career goal

    b. Marriage or career?

    c. Why I would / wouldn't like to have children

    d. An unusual plan for the future

    e. A crazy dream?

    f. The best place to live

    g. A travel plan

8 Exchange two examples of brainstorming from exercise 7 on page 82 with a partner. Answer these questions.

   a. Did the writer get a lot of ideas?

   b. Which brainstorming method gave the most ideas?

   c. Which ideas do you think are most interesting for a paragraph?

Writing focus: Review of connectors

9 Work with a partner and do the following.

- Take turns explaining what the words and expressions below mean, and how they are used.

- Write sentences for at least four of the words / expressions.

Example:

I've nearly finished my English writing textbook, Writing Paragraphs. **As a result,** *I can write very good paragraphs.*

after
and
as a result
in addition
because
before
but
consequently
for example
however
I think
in my opinion
so
therefore
when

10 With the same partner, answer these questions about connecting words and expressions.

   a. Why do writers use connectors?

   b. Should there be a connector in each sentence? Why, or why not?

   c. Which of the expressions in exercise 9 mean almost the same thing?

   d. Choose three expressions and tell about the rules for using commas with them.

   e. Which two expressions cannot start a new sentence (in academic writing)?

   f. What other connectors do you know? Make a list, and share it with another pair or the whole class.

11 Read this paragraph. With a partner, add connectors where needed. Compare your answers in groups. (There could be more than one right answer for each space.)

Changing my Future

I hope to be a successful artist someday soon. I have been painting since I was a young child a. .... all my family said I had great talent. b. .... , I couldn't get a job as an artist or make enough money selling my art. I really want to be an artist, c. .... I need to make some changes to achieve my dream. First, I plan to study for a graduate degree in Fine Art to learn more about color and to make my paintings more original. d. .... , I will have more confidence about trying to sell my work. e. .... , I am going to design a website to show and sell my paintings. If you have dreams, don't wait for fate. You have to do something yourself to achieve your dreams. Going back to school or exploring different business opportunities are just two ways to change your future.

12 Read the paragraph again to underline any future wishes and plans.

Put it together

a Use one of the topics from exercise 7 on page 82 for which you brainstormed ideas.

b Write a paragraph, using connectors and some of the future forms you practiced. Then check your writing.

c Exchange papers with a partner.
- Fill out the Peer Review Form on page 99.
- Talk with your partner and go over each form.

d Read your paragraph again and make changes to improve it.

e Hand in the second draft of your paragraph to your teacher.

Grammar for Writers

This is not a grammar book; this is a writing book. However, good writers should be able to talk about grammar. Then they can talk about their writing. If you know some basic grammar terms, you can learn how to write correct and interesting sentences more easily. You can understand, talk about, and ask questions about the grammatical mistakes you make in your writing, and you can correct them more easily. At the same time, it is important to develop a "feeling" or intuition about English grammar: you can do this by exposing yourself to English. Read English stories, magazines, and web pages. Listen to English songs; watch English movies; have conversations in English. You will be surprised at how these activities also help your writing!

Parts of Speech

⊃ **Noun**

A *noun* names something: a person or animal (*teacher, Anne, bird*), a place (*mountain, New York, bedroom*), a thing (*computer, dress, cell phone*), or idea (*love, honesty, happiness*).

Writers need to think about *noun phrases* in addition to simple nouns. A noun phrase includes the main noun and some words that describe it.

bag (noun)

The bag that my mother gave me. (noun phrase)

Note: *Pronouns* (*I, you, he, she, it, we,* and *they*) are words that replace nouns, and are used in the same way.

The topic of your sentences and paragraphs will be a noun or noun phrase.

⊃ **Verb**

The *verb* tells about the action or condition in the sentence.

He **runs**.	(action)
They **are eating** *dinner.*	

She **seems** *lonely.*	(condition)
I **feel** *tired.*	

Verbs change slightly according to who is doing the action (*he runs; they run*) and the tense or time (*he runs every day; he ran yesterday*). We say that a verb must *agree* with the person or thing that the sentence is about.

A *verb phrase* is the main verb (*run*) plus any auxiliary verbs (*does run, is running, has run, could be running*).

Verb phrases show your feelings about your topic. You also use verbs when you write to tell stories and to explain what happened.

⊃ **Preposition**

Prepositions are short words (*at, on, for*) that connect ideas. They tell about time, place, or purpose (reason).

We eat dinner **at** *seven o'clock.*   (time)
My book is **on** *the desk.* (place)
She bought a gift **for** *her friend.*   (purpose)

A *prepositional phrase* includes a preposition and a noun. The prepositional phrases in the examples above are at *seven o'clock, on the desk*, and *for her friend*.

Adding prepositional phrases to your sentences is an easy way to write longer, more detailed sentences.

⊃ **Adjective**

An *adjective* describes, or tells about, a noun. It answers the question *What kind of* or *Which?*

She has a **red** *bag.* (What kind of bag does she have?)
The **small brown** *dog is mine.* (Which dog is yours?)

Adjective phrases—several words—do the same thing. Notice that there can be several adjective phrases for one noun.

She has a bag **from Peru**.
The dog **over there by that tree** *is mine.*

Many adjective phrases are prepositional phrases. Since adjectives and adjective phrases describe nouns, you will often see adjective phrases in noun phrases:

The red bag **with the black handles** *is mine.*

Using adjectives when you write helps you paint a picture of the nouns you are describing. They help your reader to see what you are describing.

⊃ **Adverb**

An *adverb* describes, or tells about, a verb. It answers the questions *Where, When, How, For how long / How often,* and *Why?*

It rained **yesterday.**   (When did it rain?)
She eats **slowly**.   (How does she eat?)
I **sometimes** *play tennis.*   (How often do you play tennis?)

Adverb phrases contain several words. These may also be prepositional phrases. There can be more than one adverb phrase in a sentence.

She went **to the bank to get some money.** (Where did she go? Why did she go there?)

Adverbs add power to your verb phrases. They add more information and support to your ideas.

Use both adjectives and adverbs to make your writing more sophisticated, interesting, and accurate.

Article

There are three articles in English: *a, an,* and *the.* All of the articles signal nouns: *She is* **a friend**; *Would you like* **an apple**?; *Meet me in* **the classroom**. However, not all nouns have articles before them: *I will see you on* **Friday**; *I didn't see that* **movie**; *I don't believe in* **magic**. Using English articles correctly takes a lot of practice. Do not be discouraged if you make mistakes with articles while learning to write in English.

Parts of a Sentence

A complete sentence must have a subject and a predicate.

Subject

The subject of a sentence is the person, thing, or idea that the sentence is about. It is always a noun or a noun phrase. In a statement, it usually comes before the verb. To check if your subject agrees with the verb, find the *head noun*—the most basic noun that the sentence is about.

Amy *is my sister.*
She *is my sister.*
The girl *with the long hair is my sister.* (*girl* is the head noun)
The *young* **girl** *with the long hair sitting over there is my sister.* (*girl* is the head noun)

Predicate

The predicate tells what the subject does, what happens to the subject, or how the subject is. The predicate contains at least the verb, and often other words that follow the verb.

Amy **studies.**
Amy **studies English.**
Amy **studies English in her room for several hours every night.**

Finding the subject and predicate of your sentences helps you see whether you have a complete sentence, and whether the subject and verb of your sentence agree.

Punctuation

Here are some common rules for using punctuation in your writing. Of course, this is not a complete list. If you have further questions, check a grammar book or ask your teacher.

⊃ **Capitalization**

Always capitalize:
- the first word of every sentence.
- days of the week (*Tuesday*) and months of the year (*April*).
- the first letter (only) of the names of people and places (*Bangkok, Ayaka Seo*).
- the main words of a title, but not articles (*a, an, the*) or prepositions (words like *to, of, for*) or conjunctions (*and, but*), unless they are the first word in the title: *The Three Things I Do in the Morning.*

⊃ **Period (.)**

A period comes at the end of a statement:
An electronic dictionary is more convenient than a paper one.

If the sentence ends with an abbreviation, don't use more than one period:
RIGHT: *My mother just finished her Ph.D.*
WRONG: *My mother just finished her Ph.D..*

⊃ **Comma (,)**

Use a comma to separate a series of three or more items:
I take a dictionary, a notebook, and some paper to class every day.

Use a comma before words like *and, but, or,* and *so* to separate two parts of a sentence that each have a subject and a verb.
She needed some work experience, so she got a part-time job.
He did not study at all, but he still got an 87 on the test.

Use a comma after an introductory word or expression, such as *However, Therefore,* and *In conclusion*:
However, the high price of electric cars means that most people cannot afford one.

⊃ **Quotation marks (" ")**

Use quotation marks when you type or write the title of a book or movie:
"Hamlet" was written by Shakespeare.

When you use a word processor, you can use italics instead:
Hamlet was written by Shakespeare.

Use quotation marks to show the exact words someone spoke or wrote:
The professor announced, "We're going to have an exam next week."
Shakespeare wrote, "All the world's a stage."

Do not use quotation marks if you're reporting what another person said:
The professor said that we should study hard this week.

⊃ Punctuation when using quotation marks

If you are using expressions like *he said* or *the girl remarked* after the quotation, then use a comma and not a period at the end of the quoted sentence:
"We're going to have an exam next week," announced the professor.

Use a period if the quoted sentence comes at the end:
The professor announced, "We're going to have an exam next week."

Notice how a comma is used after *announced*, above, to introduce the quotation.

⊃ Quotation marks and capitalization

Capitalize the first letter of the word that begins a quotation. However, if an expression like *she said* interrupts the quotation and divides the sentence, then do not capitalize the first word of the part that finishes the quotation:
"Next week," said the professor, "we are going to have an exam."

The comma after *week* separates the quotation from the rest of the sentence.

Use a capital letter only if the second part is a new, complete sentence:
"We'll have an exam next week," explained the teacher. "It will take thirty minutes."

⊃ Advice for academic writing

The following are not usually used in academic writing, although they are fine in informal situations, such as letters to your friends.

- Parentheses that give information which is not part of your main sentence:
Smart phones are useful (and besides, I think they look great).

  If your idea is important, it should be in a sentence of its own. If it is not important, it should not be in your paper.

- The abbreviation *etc.* to continue a list. Instead, use a phrase like *such as* in your sentence:
Students in my university come from countries such as China, India, and Australia.

- Exclamation points (!). Instead, write strong sentences with plenty of details to show your reader your feelings:
Angel Falls is one of the most spectacular natural wonders you will ever see.

- An ellipsis (…) at the end of a sentence, to show that the sentence is not finished:
The professor said that I should study hard, so …

  Instead, finish your sentence:

  The professor said that I should study hard, so I should not go to the party tonight.

Sample paragraph: Brainstorming

<u>Assignment</u>: Write a paragraph about a person who is important to you. Explain why that person is special. Use a word map to brainstorm ideas, edit your map, and then write your first draft. Then exchange papers with a classmate and fill out a Peer Review Form. After you receive your classmate's form, write a second draft using ideas from your classmate and your own ideas.

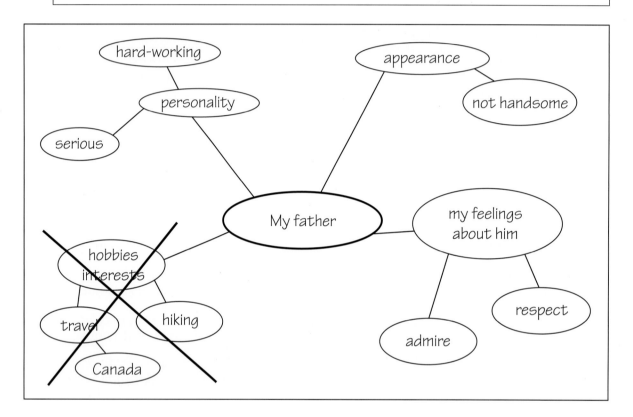

Sample paragraph: First draft

Kensaku Isagawa

May 11, 2011

Writing Class

Instructor: Carlos Islam

1st Draft

I admire many things about my father. He does not have any special qualities. He would be easy to overlook because he is not special. He is a good person. I get bored when I work with him. He has strong opinions, and he is tough and generous to other peoples. He always looks at the future. He never regrets something. I learned a lot from him.

Peer Review Form

Writer's name: Kensaku Isagawa

Reviewer's name: Yumika Hara

Title: ?

Date: May 12, 2011

1. What is the topic of the paragraph? What is the writer's opinion about that topic?

Topic = Ken's father   Opinion = Ken admires his father

2. Look at the word map. Were any ideas crossed out? Why, do you think?

Yes, he crossed out "hobbies." I don't know why, but maybe there were too many ideas for one paragraph. "Hobbies" is not why he admires his father, I guess.

3. Read the paragraph again. What is the topic sentence? Write it here.

I admire many things about (my father.)

Circle the topic and underline the main idea.

4. How many supporting sentences are there?

seven

5. Is there a concluding sentence? If so, what does it do (for example, restate the topic sentence, give advice, make a prediction, offer a final comment)?

Yes, it offers a final comment.

6. Which sentence is your favourite? Write it here.

He has strong opinions, and he is tough and generous to other peoples.

7. Do you have any questions or comments for the writer?

This is interesting. I want to know more about your father. Also, I think it is better to be specific. Why is he a "good" person and why isn't he "special"?

I think the sentence, "I get bored when I work with him" is not connected to your idea. The concluding sentence would be stronger if you said what you learned from your father, or if said something like, "I hope I can be like my father when I have children." Also, I want to know what doesn't he regret? Can you tell me examples? What have you learned from him?

Sample paragraph: Final draft

Kensaku Isagawa

May 15, 2011

Writing Class

Instructor: Carlos Islam

I Respect My Father

I admire many things about my father, but he does not have any special qualities. He would be easy to overlook because he is not outstandingly handsome or striking in appearance. However, he is a careful, serious, and hard working person. He has strong opinions, and he is tough and generous to other people. He always looks to the future. He never regrets anything. I think I learned a lot from him.

Peer Review Form—Unit 5

Writer's name: ....

Reviewer's name: ....

Title: ....

Date: ....

1. What is the topic of the paragraph? What is the writer's opinion about that topic?

2. Look at the freewriting. Is it long or short? Have any ideas been crossed out? Why, do you think?

3. Read the paragraph again. What is the topic sentence? Write it here.

    ....

    ....

    Circle the topic and underline the main idea.

4. How many supporting sentences are there?

5. Is there a concluding sentence? If so, what does it do (for example, restate the topic sentence, give advice, make a prediction, offer a final comment)?

6. Does the paragraph have these things?

	yes	no
• writer's name and date		
• paragraph title		
• descriptive adjectives		
• some sentences or adjectives combined with *and*		
• some sentences or adjectives combined with *but*		

7. Do you have any questions or comments for the writer?

92 ADDITIONAL MATERIALS

Peer Review Form—Unit 6

Writer's name: ....

Reviewer's name: ....

Title: ....

Date: ....

1. What is the topic of the paragraph? What is the writer's opinion about that topic?

2. Read the paragraph again. What is the topic sentence? Write it here.

   ....

   ....

   Circle the topic and underline the main idea.

3. How many supporting sentences are there?

4. Underline supporting sentences that state an opinion.

5. Double underline sentences that support an opinion.

6. How many sentences state facts?

7. Is there a concluding sentence? If so, what does it do (for example, restate the topic sentence, make a prediction, give a suggestion)?

8. Which sentence is your favorite? Write it here.

   ....

   ....

9. Do you have any questions or comments for the writer?

Peer Review Form—Unit 7

Writer's name: ....

Reviewer's name: ....

Title: ....

Date: ....

1. What is the topic of the paragraph?

2. Look at the brainstorming.
   a. What kind of brainstorming did the writer use?
   b. Was the brainstorming edited?
   c. Do you think that method helped the writer think of a lot of ideas?

3. Read the paragraph again.
   a. What do you think about the writer's explanation or excuse?
   b. Would you make the same choice, do you think? Why, or why not?

4. <u>Underline</u> the topic sentence.

5. Did the writer combine any sentences with *so* or *because?* If so, write them here.
   ....
   ....
   ....

6. Which sentence is your favorite? Write it here.
   ....
   ....

7. Do you have any questions or comments for the writer?

Peer Review Form—Unit 8

Writer's name: ....

Reviewer's name: ....

Title: ....

Date: ....

1. What is the topic? What problem does the writer explain?

2. Look at the writer's list.

   a. Which idea do you think is the most important?

   b. Were any ideas crossed out? Why, do you think?

   c. Did the writer number his / her ideas in order of importance?

3. Read the paragraph again. What is the topic sentence? Write it here.

   ....

   ....

   (Circle) the topic and <u>underline</u> the main idea.

4. How many supporting sentences are there?

5. Is there a concluding sentence? If so, what does it do?

6. Write the last supporting sentence. Is it the most important supporting idea?

   ....

   ....

7. Does the paragraph have these things?

	yes	no
• at least three supporting ideas		
• supporting sentences expressing desire or obligation		

8. Do you have any questions or comments for the writer?

Peer Review Form—Unit 9

Writer's name: ....

Reviewer's name: ....

Title: ....

Date: ....

1. What is the topic of the paragraph?

2. Write one or two words to describe the feeling or mood of the narrative (for example, *scary, strange, happy, sad*).

3. Look at the brainstorming.
   a. What kind of brainstorming did the writer use?
   b. Was the brainstorming edited?
   c. Do you think that method helped the writer think of a lot of ideas?

4. Read the paragraph again. Make a list of the main events, in the order they happened.

5. Is there a concluding sentence? If so, what does it do?

6. Which sentence is your favorite? Write it here.

   ....

   ....

7. Does the paragraph have these things?

	yes	no
• some sentences or adjectives combined with *after*		
• some sentences or adjectives combined with *before*		
• some sentences or adjectives combined with *when*		

8. Do you have any questions or comments for the writer?

Peer Review Form—Unit 10

Writer's name: ....

Reviewer's name: ....

Title: ....

Date: ....

1. What two things is the writer comparing? What is the writer's opinion about each of the things?

2. Look at the double list the writer used to brainstorm.
   a. Was it long or short?
   b. Which ideas were used?
   c. Were they the most interesting to you?

3. Read the paragraph again. What is the topic sentence? Write it here.

   ....

   ....

   Circle the topic and underline the main idea.

4. How many supporting sentences are there?

5. Is there a concluding sentence? If so, what does it do?

6. Does the paragraph have these things?

	yes	no
• point-by-point style		
• block style		
• two ideas joined using *whereas*		
• two ideas joined using *however*		

7. Do you have any questions or comments for the writer?

PHOTOCOPIABLE

Peer Review Form—Unit 11

Writer's name: ....

Reviewer's name: ....

Title: ....

Date: ....

1. What is the difficult decision the writer made? Why was it difficult?

2. What is the topic sentence? Write it here.

   ....

   ....

3. Did the writer begin with a question? If so, how did you answer it?

4. Read the paragraph again. <u>Underline</u> the words and expressions the writer used to link sentences and ideas (such as *and*, *but*, *because*, *so*, *therefore*, *as a result*, *consequently*).

   Do you think the writer used commas correctly in those sentences? If you are not sure, make a star (*) next to the sentence.

5. Was it easy to understand the paragraph? Were all the events told in a logical order?

6. Is there a concluding sentence? If so, what does it do?

7. Which sentence is your favorite? Write it here.

   ....

   ....

8. Do you have any questions or comments for the writer?

Peer Review Form—Unit 12

Writer's name: ....

Reviewer's name: ....

Title: ....

Date: ....

1. What is the topic of the paragraph? What is the writer's opinion about that topic?

2. Look at the brainstorming.
   a. Would you have used a different technique? Why, or why not?
   b. Did the writer get a lot of ideas from the brainstorming?

3. Read the paragraph again. What does the writer hope or desire for the future?

4. How many supporting sentences are there?

5. Do the supporting sentences include any of these things?

	yes	no
• connecting words and expressions		
• facts		
• opinions		
• examples		

6. Is there a concluding sentence? If so, what does it do?

7. Which sentence is your favorite? Write it here.

   ....

   ....

8. Do you have any questions or comments for the writer?

PHOTOCOPIABLE

Macmillan Education
4 Crinan Street
London N1 9XW
A division of Macmillan Publishers Limited
Companies and representatives throughout the
world

ISBN 978-0-230-41593-5

Text © Dorothy E Zemach & Carlos Islam 2011

Design and illustration © Macmillan Publishers
Limited 2011

Written by Dorothy E Zemach & Carlos Islam

First published 2005

Original design by Amanda Easter Design Ltd
Page make-up by xen
Illustrated by Jackson Graham, Sophie Grillet,
Stuart Perry
Cover design by xen based on a design by Jackie Hill
at 320 Design

Authors' acknowledgements
Thanks to students in the Intensive English
Institute at The University of Maine, especially
Kensaku Isagawa, who kindly helped pilot many
of the exercises in the book and provided helpful
comments and suggestions.
Special thanks to Tony Garside, Helen Holwill, and
David Williamson.

The publishers would like to thank the following for
their assistance in the development of this course:
Chris Cottam, Richard J. Kelly, Camella Lieske,
David Parker, Gordon Robson, Maria-Luiza Santos

The authors and publishers would like to thank
the following for permission to reproduce their
photographs:
Alamy pp25, 45, 55;
Bananastock pp13, 17(l), 29(b), 54;
Corbis pp14, 34;
Getty pp6, 29(c), 31, 36, 44, 59, 62;
Photodisc p17(r), 29(a, d);
Superstock pp20, 84.

Printed and bound in Thailand

2020 2019 2018 2017
13 12 11 10 9 8